INDONESIA:

The Sukarno Years

INDONESIA:

The Sukarno Years

Edited by Hal Kosut

FACTS ON FILE   **NEW YORK**

INDONESIA: The Sukarno Years

Library of Congress Catalog Card No.: 67-29073
ISBN 0-87196-167-9

9   8   7   6   5   4   3

PRINTED IN THE UNITED STATES OF AMERICA

N 106

CONTENTS

i

INTRODUCTION

INDONESIA, THE WORLD'S LARGEST chain of islands, stretches along the equator for 3,400 miles from northwestern Sumatra, west of the Malay Peninsula, to and including West New Guinea (also called West Irian or Irian Barat). Comprising more than 3,000 islands ranging in size from a few acres to Indonesian Borneo (Kalimantan), almost as large as France, Indonesia has a population of about 105.3 million.

Indonesia has a total land area of 734,884 square miles, and it is the 3rd largest country in Asia (after India and mainland China). The northernmost islands are only 100 miles from the Philippines; those in the south are separated from the northern coast of Australia by the narrow Timor and Arafura Seas. The Greater Sunda Islands (a term no longer officially used) include Java, Sumatra, Celebes and Borneo. The Lesser Sundas, which stretch from Bali in the west to Timor, are now officially Nusa Tenggara (Southeastern Islands). The Moluccas comprise Halmahera, Buru, Ceram and Amboina. The coasts of Java, Sumatra and Borneo are lined with tidal swamps, some of which stretch far into the interior. The only extensive dry flatlands are those of Java and Central Sumatra. The other islands are made up largely of either heavily forested rolling hills and mountains or humid morasses covered with dense vegetation.

The population ranges ethnically from Malay in the west to Oceanic Negroid in the east. The major ethnic groups are the Javanese, Sundanese, Balinese, Achinese, Bataks, Amdurese, Ambonese, Menadonese, Buginese and Dayaks. About 1¼ million people of Chinese ancestry also live in Indonesia. The Javanese constitute about 45% of the total population, the Sundanese about 15%.

1

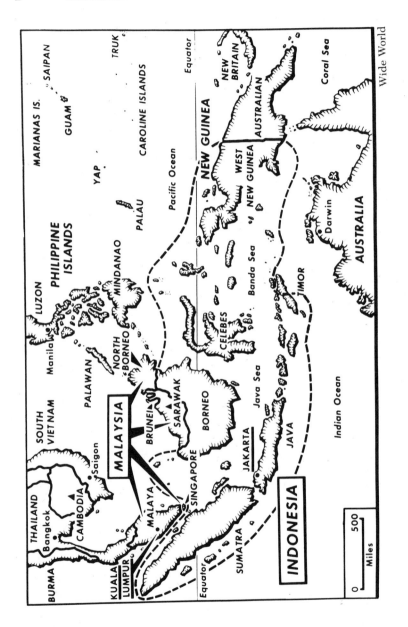

Wide World

Bahsa Indonesia is the official language. It is based primarily on Malay but contains many words from other Indonesian dialects and also from Dutch, English, Arabic, Sanskrit and other languages.

About 90% of Indonesians observe the Islamic religion. Bali's more than 1 million inhabitants are Hindu in religion and culture. The Chinese largely follow a form of Buddhism-Confuscianism. There are 3 million Christians, 70% of whom are Protestants. The principal Christian centers are in Amboina and its adjacent islands, northern Sulawesi, north-central Sumatra and Timor and the adjacent islands.

Indonesia is the world's 2d largest producer of rubber and tin, which account for more than half of its total exports. Other products are tobacco, sugar, palm oil and tea. More than 70% of all exports are produced in Sumatra, about 14% in Java. More than 1/2 the national income is derived from subsistence farming, forestry and fishing. The chief farm crop is rice, which is Indonesia's major food staple.

Indonesia is divided into 19 provinces plus the special autonomous district of Jogjakarta and the metropolitan district of Jakarta-Raya, both in Java.

Indonesia came under strong Buddhist and Hindu influence with the arrival of traders from India early in the Christian era. Native empires began to emerge with firm roots in the Buddhist and Hindu religions. The Buddhist kingdom of Sri Vijaya, established in Sumatra by the 7th Century, became the first important political center of Indonesia. The focus of political power shifted to Java by the 13th Century with the establishment of the Hindu kingdom of Majapahit in 1292. The Majapahit kingdom was paramount for 2 centuries, but its powers began to wane in the early 15th Century as the Islamic religion, brought to Indonesia by Arab traders, gained adherents. By the end of the 16th Century Islam had replaced Buddhism and Hinduism as the dominant religion of Indonesia.

Under Islamic rule, Indonesia split up into small and weak states powerless to resist Western colonialist infiltration. The Portuguese arrived in Indonesia early in the 16th Century and established trading posts. They were followed by the Dutch in 1596 and the British in 1600. British-Netherlands rivalry intensified in the early 17th Century with the formation of the Dutch East India Company in 1602 and the English East India Company. The Dutch soon ousted the Portuguese, who were permitted to retain only the eastern part of Timor.

Turning full attention to their remaining rivals, the Dutch clashed repeatedly with the British between 1610 and 1623 but finally ousted them and became the unchallenged colonial power in Indonesia. The Dutch East India Company expanded its control throughout Indonesia in the 17th and 18th Centuries. The Dutch government took over the company's holdings after the firm was liquidated in 1799. Indonesia then became known alternately as the Netherlands East Indies, the Netherland East Indies, Netherland India or the Dutch East Indies.

Dutch rule was interrupted briefly during the Napoleonic Wars (1811-15) when the British returned. But the Dutch strengthened their hold over Indonesia throughout the 19th Century by intensifying the exploitation of the islands' natural resources and by widening their political control.

Colonialism in Indonesia faced its first serious challenge in 1825 when Prince Diponegoro of Java launched a long and bloody but unsuccessful war to oust the Dutch. Futile rebellions were also carried out against the Dutch by native rulers of Bali in 1906 and 1908.

Indonesia's struggle for independence entered a new phase in 1927 with the creation of a political movement called the Nationalist Party. The party was established and headed by Indonesia's leading proponent of ousting the Dutch — Dr. Achmed Sukarno (Soekarno in the original Dutch spelling; in accordance with Javanese custom, Sukarno does not use his given name of Achmed). Mohammed Hatta was Sukarno's principal collaborator in forming the party. The party, on its formation, represented an amalgamation of several leftwing groups that had sought to overthrow the Dutch in 1926 but were suppressed. The party was modeled after the Congress Party of India and followed the Indian practice of boycotts and non-cooperation.

The Dutch moved early to suppress this new outgrowth of

Sukarno in 1962 at height of his power (Wide World photo)

Indonesian aspiration for freedom by arresting Nationalist Party followers. Sukarno countered by organizing "fighting squads" to resist the Dutch. Sukarno's revolutionary activities resulted in his arrest in 1929. He was brought to trial in 1930 and imprisoned for 2 years. On ending his jail term, Sukarno was exiled in 1932 to Endeh, in the Lesser Sunda islands. In 1933 Dutch authorities transferred him to Sumatra.

Dutch rule was suspended when Japanese forces captured the islands in 1942 during the early stages of the Pacific phase of World War II. With the Japanese in control, anti-nationalist measures that had been instituted by the Dutch were eased. The Japanese interned the Dutch and Eurasians and permitted Bahsa Indonesia to replace Dutch as the official language. The Japanese released Sukarno from his Sumatra detention in 1942 and freed other Indonesian nationalist followers.

Although Sukarno's anti-Japanese sentiments were well known, he agreed to cooperate with the Japanese occupation forces, apparently to maintain contact with his underground followers. Sukarno was elected president of the Japanese-sponsored Java Central Council in 1943. He accepted a Japanese invitation to visit Tokyo, where Emperor Hirohito bestowed on him the order of Sacred Treasure, 2d Class. One of Sukarno's duties in the puppet administration was to recruit Indonesian laborers to work on Japanese projects.

Sukarno's answer to those who criticized him for cooperating with Indonesia's conquerors: "Every Javanese understands why I collaborated with the Japanese. The Japanese tried to use the Indonesians for their own purposes and let us prepare for our independence under false promises. But we turned the tables on them. We prepared for the hour of liberty . . . no power on earth can take it away from us."

Sukarno was born June 6, 1901 in Blitar, Java. He obtained his secondary school education in Surabaya, Java. From there he went on to the Technical Engineering College in Bandung, from which he received a degree in civil engineering. He indicated later that his resentment of racial slurs he encountered while a student had helped determine the course of his political career.

Sukarno, whose aspirations apparently included an ambition to head a coalition of uncommitted nations that would hold the balance of power between the Communist and non-Communist worlds, considered himself above all a revolutionary. In his Independence Day speech Aug. 17, 1960 he told fellow Indonesians: "I belong to that group of people who are bound in spiritual longing by the romanticism of revolution. I am inspired by it. I am fascinated by it. I am completely absorbed by it. I am obsessed by [it]. . . . That is why I, who have been given the topmost leadership in the struggle of the Indonesian nation, never tire of appealing and exhorting: solve our national problems in a revolutionary way, make the revolutionary spirit surge on, see to it that the fire of our revolution does not die or grow dim, not even for a single moment. Come, then, keep burning the flames of the leaping fire of revolution! Brothers and sisters, let us become logs to feed the fire of revolution!"

By the late 1940s and throughout the 1950s Sukarno was regarded by most Indonesians as the living symbol of their independence and nationhood. An orator of exceptional brilliance and magnetism, he found it possible to persuade his people for years that all Indonesia's troubles were caused by colonialist and imperialist exploitation. Glorying in the self-assumed title Bung (brother) Karno, he assured his followers that Allah had chosen him to lead Indonesia along a vaguely Leftist path to greatness.

By the 1960s, however, he was beginning to lose some of the public favor as grumbling grew about his waste of government money, his bureaucratic inefficiency, his personal ostentation, his imperiousness and his continuing cordial relations with the Communists.

CAMPAIGN FOR INDEPENDENCE

1945-49

When World War II ended in Aug. 1945, Indonesian nationalists proclaimed a provisional republican government with the charismatic Sukarno as president. Dutch and Allied forces landed on Java the following month, and 4 years of military and diplomatic struggle followed before sovereignty was finally conferred by the Dutch on an independent United States of Indonesia headed by Sukarno.

The Dutch-Indonesian confrontation was marked by repeated armed clashes and truces. Major diplomatic steps included: the Malino Conference, which called for a federated USI (United States of Indonesia) within the framework of the Netherlands kingdom; the Linggadjati Agreement, under which the Dutch agreed to recognize the Indonesian republic as a sovereign state and to work with it to create a USI and a Netherlands-Indonesian Union; and the *Renville* Agreement, which amplified the Linggadjati Agreement's political terms and provided for a truce.

The UN took up the dispute in 1947, and the UN Security Council began efforts to end the fighting and to arrange a political settlement. A Security Council-appointed UN Committee of Good Offices (CGO) worked with both sides and proved successful in helping to halt military clashes. The CGO was succeeded by a UN Commission for Indonesia, which continued to represent the Security Council and proved useful in the Dutch-Indonesian negotiations that eventually resulted in Indonesian independence.

Indonesians Form Provisional Republic; Dutch & Allies Return

The capitulation of Japanese military forces in Indonesia and other areas of the Pacific Aug. 15, 1945 marked the end of

World War II and the emergence of Indonesia's long-smoldering nationalist movement as a powerful political force. Taking advantage of the vacuum created by the surrender of Japanese troops in the Indonesian islands and the absence of a Dutch colonial government, the nationalists proclaimed a "Provisional Indonesian Republican Government" in Jogjakarta, Java Aug. 17, 1945.

The Jogjakarta regime claimed jurisdiction over the islands of Java, Sumatra and Madura. A nationalist-appointed Independence Committee named Sukarno president and Mohammed Hatta vice president. A cabinet was formed later in August with Sutan Sjahrir as prime minister. The republican government stated that its purpose was to achieve complete independence.

The Netherlands reestablished its official presence on Java when a small number of Dutch troops, accompanying a larger force of British and Indian soldiers, landed on the island Sept. 28, 1945. The Allied force occupied Batavia, the capital city and seat of Dutch administration. In a proclamation issued Sept. 29, Lord Louis Mountbatten, Allied supreme commander in Southeast Asia, declared that the Allied force had returned to Java to accept the surrender of the Japanese troops and to hold the island until the Netherlands East Indies (NEI) government resumed control. Mountbatten authorized the Japanese soldiers to assist in maintaining public order until they were relieved by Allied troops.

The Allied commander in Java, British Lt. Gen. Sir Philip Christinson, said in Batavia Sept. 28 that the government established by Sukarno would not be ousted and that it would be expected to govern in areas not taken over by Allied forces. Christinson promised that the Allies would not disarm the Indonesian conscripts who had been trained by the Japanese for internal security or take away the weapons of the Soeka-rillas, a body of nationalist volunteers.

The Netherlands' immediate reaction to the establishment of the Indonesian republic had been adamant opposition. A statement issued in The Hague Oct. 1 said the Netherlands would not recognize the regime nor negotiate with it because Sukarno had "allowed himself to be the tool and puppet of the Japanese" during the occupation. Sukarno had "systematically preached hatred aginst the Allies," the statement said. Netherlands Colonial Min. J. J. Logeman had charged Sept. 30 that Sukarno's "Japanese puppet government" had been formed "while the Japanese military forces still exercised control in Java." Sukarno Oct. 14 called for a Moslem "holy war against the Dutch infidel."

Netherlands East Indies (NEI) Gov. Hubertus J. van Mook said in Batavia Oct. 15 that the Dutch government would be willing to negotiate with the Indonesian leaders. But only, he declared, if they first called a halt to a campaign of violence they had launched against Allied forces early in October. Referring to the 100,000 persons interned during the Japanese occupation, van Mook insisted that the nationalists release the internees.

Vice Pres. Hatta listed the nationalists' goals Oct. 18. He said: (a) Dutch troop reinforcements must be barred from Java, and Dutch troops already there must be removed; (b) the Netherlands Indies Civil Affairs Administration, which, he claimed, was returning under force of Allied arms to reestablish Dutch control, must not be allowed to function; (c) the Indonesian-Dutch dispute over nationalist demands for independence should be turned over to an international body for mediation. In the meantime, the Dutch should extend *de facto* recognition to the Sukarno government.

The landing of Allied forces on Java Sept. 28, 1945 had precipitated military resistance by the Indonesians. Armed nationalists attacked British, Indian and Dutch forces throughout the island during the first days of October. The nationalists also fought Japanese troops who complied with the Allied directive to hold their positions. The disorders were intensified by Indonesian extremists, who, acting independently of the nationalists, also attacked Allied soldiers. Sukarno denounced the actions of the extremists.

Fighting continued through most of October, and bloody battles raged in Batavia, Bandung, Jogjakarta and Surabaya. Casualties were heavy on both sides. The Japanese, particularly, suffered heavy losses.

The intensity of anti-Dutch feeling was reflected in "a declaration of war" against the Dutch, Eurasians and Ambonese issued Oct. 13 by a group identifying itself as the "Hq. of the Indonesian People's Army." A major portion of the Netherlands East Indies army was recruited from Amboina.) The People's Army proclamation accused the British of "giving protection to the return of the Dutch administration." The Allies reacted by placing Batavia under military rule.

The Javanese unrest was temporarily suppressed after more Allied troops landed on the island in mid-October. Allied soldiers recaptured Surabaya and relieved the Japanese of control of Bandung, which they had retaken from extremists Oct. 12. An Allied military statement Oct. 20 said that with the exception of the principal centers in Java taken over by British troops, "the whole of Java is in the hands of the Indonesians and is claimed to be administrated by Sukarno's government."

Allied-Indonesian fighting erupted again in Java Jan. 8, 1946 and continued through November. The fighting spread to other Indonesian islands, including Sumatra and Celebes. The most serious clashes occurred during August and the early part of September. In one of the major incidents reported from Java, Allied authorities said Aug. 11 that in the previous 5 days more than 300 Indonesians had been killed around Semarang and 75 had been slain in the Bandung area.

Dutch troops assumed greater responsibility in the drive to pacify Java and Sumatra towards the end of 1946 as the Netherlands continued to send more troop reinforcements to the islands. The entire British-Indian occupation force withdrew from the Indonesian islands Nov. 29, leaving the Dutch army alone to cope with the unrest.

The decision to withdraw the Indian and British troops had been announced by Allied headquarters in Batavia Sept. 7. In announcing the Nov. 30 pull-out date, the statement said that by that date the Allies would have fulfilled their 2-fold mission: the evacuation of Allied war prisoners and internees and the disarming of the Japanese troops.

At Britain's urging, the Netherlands agreed to meet with Indonesian leaders to seek a solution to the political turmoil.

In the first Dutch-Indonesian contact, NEI Gov. van Mook held informal discussions with a republican delegation headed by Sukarno in Batavia Oct. 28, 1945. A statement issued by van Mook Nov. 5 outlined the Netherlands' policy on Indonesia. It said that the Netherlands recognized "the legitimate aspirations of Indonesians to national existence" and that the Netherlands would seek "the rapid development of Indonesia as a partner" in a commonwealth of other Dutch territories in other parts of the world.

The Batavia conference was followed by the first round of formal talks between Dutch and Indonesian representatives in Gelderland, the Netherlands Apr. 9-24, 1946. But no agreement was reached.

Colonial Min. Logeman conceded May 2 that Sukarno's regime "is regarded as being representative of the national aim even by those who would have nothing to do with the republic." But he said the Dutch insisted that the Indonesian islands other than Java "should be able to express their own will as to their future status with Indonesia."

A series of counter-proposals were sent by Premier Sjahrir to Gov. van Mook June 17, 1946. They included demands for: (a) a treaty under which the Netherlands would grant "*de facto* recognition*" to the republican government; (b) a cease-fire, with both Indonesian and Dutch forces retaining their respective positions; (c) Dutch cooperation in the establishment of an Indonesian Free State that would include the islands not in the republic.

Sjahrir Kidnaped, then Released; New Cabinet Formed

Premier Sjahrir was kidnaped June 27, 1946 by armed extremists at Solo, Java. He was seized together with an Indonesian delegation (including 2 other cabinet ministers) that was en route to Batavia to resume political negotiations with Gov. van Mook. Republican army troops secured the release of Sjahrir and his party July 1.

Sukarno had assumed all powers of government following Sjahrir's abduction, pending restoration of the normal functions of government. A state of emergency was declared, and the government launched a purge of the Indonesian army. The emergency was declared ended Aug. 13. Sukarno relinquished his emergency powers, and parliamentary government was reinstituted.

In August Sukarno asked Sjahrir to form a new cabinet. Its formation was announced Oct. 2. For the first time since the republic's founding Indonesia's cabinet included all major parties and representatives of Indonesian minorities. The parties represented were the Socialists (PSI), Sukarno's National Party (PNI) and the Moslem Masjumi party. Premier Sjahrir assumed the additional post of foreign minister, and Amir Sjarifuddin was named defense minister; both were PSI members.

Dutch Sponsor Malino Conference

The Netherlands sponsored a conference at Malino, Celebes July 16-24, 1946 to determine the future status of the Netherlands East Indies territories. The conferees adopted a resolution proposing the establishment of a federated "United States of Indonesia" (USI) within the framework of the Netherlands kingdom. The USI was to comprise 4 parts: Borneo, Java, Sumatra and the so-called "Great East Territories," which included the smaller islands of the Indonesian archipelago. A future conference was to determine (a) how long the USI and the Netherlands government should continue to cooperate with each other, and (b) whether to establish a permanent USI-Dutch relationship.

The Indonesian republic was not represented at the Malino conference. Attending the meeting were representatives of all other Netherlands East Indies territories, including Borneo, Celebes, Bali, Lombok, Moluccas and West New Guinea.

Dutch authorities announced Aug. 24 that an Advisory Council for Borneo & The Great East Territories had been established in Batavia. The council consisted of 6 Dutch officials and the 7 Indonesian members of the Commission General for Borneo & the Great East Territories. Bali had joined the Great East Territories state Aug. 10.

Dutch & Indonesians Negotiate Truce

Dutch and Indonesian negotiators agreed Oct. 14, 1946 to a truce between Allied and Indonesian forces. The cease-fire was worked out at resumed talks held in Batavia under British auspices. The pact provided for: (a) a halt in the fighting while both sides retained their military positions; (b) establishment of a Joint Truce Commission, which would supervise the technical aspects of enforcing the truce.

At the time of the cease-fire, Dutch forces were in complete control of almost all of east and west Java, almost the entire northern coastline and the port of Tjilatjap on the south coast. Republican forces retained control of a major portion of south and south-central Java and a wide area around Jogjakarta. Dutch control of Sumatra was confined to the areas around Medan, Palembang and Padang; most of Madura was occupied by the Dutch.

The Netherlands agreed Nov. 15, 1946 to the recognition of the Indonesian republic as a sovereign state, to the establishment of a United States of Indonesia (USI) and to the creation of a Netherlands-Indonesian Union. The agreement took the form of a draft plan signed that day by Dutch and Indonesian negotiators in Linggadjati, Java. The pact, called the Linggadjati Agreement, required ratification by the parliaments of both countries before it could take effect. The agreement contained the essential elements proposed at the Malino Conference.

Principal points of the agreement: The Netherlands recognized the Indonesian Republic "as exercising *de facto* authority over Java, Madura and Sumatra. The areas occupied by Allied or Dutch forces in those 3 islands shall be included gradually . . . in republican territory." The Netherlands and the republic would establish "a sovereign democratic state on a federal basis, to be called the United States of Indonesia." The states that would comprise the USI were: the republic, Borneo and East Indonesia, which included Celebes, Bali, the Moluccas and the other smaller islands. The Netherlands and the republic would cooperate in the establishment of a Netherlands-Indonesian Union, which would comprise the USI, the Netherlands and its West Indies colonies of Surinam and Curacao. The USI and the union would be created before Jan. 1, 1949. A Constituent Assembly, represented by delegates of the republic and other USI territories, would draw up a constitution for the USI. The Netherlands and republican governments would establish a joint body to settle any future disputes that might arise over the Linggadjati Agreement. If joint consultations failed, the matter would be submitted to a 3d nation or to the World Court if 3d-nation arbitration proved unsuccessful.

The talks in Linggadjati had started Nov. 12. The meetings had been preceded by a round of negotiations in Batavia Nov. 4-7. A Netherlands government statement issued at the conclusion of the earlier conference had indicated that Dutch opposition to Sukarno would not stand in the way of an agreement with the republic. The statement said: The Netherlands "no longer considers it to be conducive to fruitful consultation that the distinction between Premier Sjahrir, who could be included in the discussions, and Pres. Sukarno, who could not, should be maintained. Since the republic is a fact of political reality at the present moment, the government accepts its organization as it is."

The Dutch parliament approved the Linggadjati Agreement Dec. 20.

Fighting Renewed, Linggadjati Agreement Collapses

Only 10 days after Dutch parliamentary approval of the Linggadjati Agreement, Dutch troops launched "large-scale action" against Indonesian forces in the Medan area of Sumatra Dec. 30, 1946. The Dutch authorities in Batavia said the Indonesians had repeatedly violated the Oct. 14 truce agreement in Medan and other areas of Sumatra and Java. Indonesian Defense Min. Sjarifuddin, denying the charges, claimed that Indonesian forces had been "provoked daily" by the Dutch.

In resuming military operations, Dutch troops during the first week of Jan. 1947 overcame strong Indonesian resistance in Medan and cleared the defense perimeter around the city. The Dutch scored similar successes against Indonesians in the Bandung and Semarang sectors of Java.

Dutch and Indonesian officials conferred in an effort to end the renewed fighting, and a new cease-fire was announced by negotiators Feb. 14.

The Linggadjati Agreement was formally signed by Dutch and Indonesian representatives in Batavia Mar. 25, 1947. The signing had been delayed by disagreement over the agreement's meaning. In an effort to resolve the divergent views and pave the way for the pact's implementation, Dutch and Indonesian republican officials had resumed negotiations Jan. 22. The deadlock appeared to have been broken, as evidenced by the signing of the document Mar. 25. But during a subsequent exchange of views (between Mar. 24 and July 18) both sides reverted to their opposing interpretations of the Linggadjati Agreement. As a result, negotiations broke down completely; the Dutch then resumed full-scale military action against republican forces July 20.

Basic differences over the Linggadjati Agreement were reflected in a Dutch note of May 27 and an Indonesian reply June 7.

The note handed to an Indonesian republican delegation May 27 recapitulated the Netherlands government's position. It said: (a) In view of the fact that the Oct. 14, 1946 truce agreement had not been honored by republican forces, joint Dutch-Indonesian measures must be taken to implement the Linggadjati Agreement by ending the "acts of violence." The Netherlands considered that a "reduction of military forces on both sides" would be the best means of achieving peace. (b) Pending the formation of the United States of Indonesia, Dutch control during the interim period must be maintained on a *de jure* basis. (c) Public order should be maintained by a joint force of Dutch and Indonesian police. (d) The Netherlands would be responsible for the defense of Indonesia by keeping its army on the islands "pending the build-up of modern Indonesian armed forces."

Main points of the republican communication submitted to the Dutch June 7: (a) The republic accepted the principle of an interim government for the United States of Indonesia, but it insisted that "at least 1/2 the members of this government" should include republican representatives; the other 1/2 should be drawn from East Indonesia and Borneo. (b) The future status of East Indonesia had been determined "independently of the will of the people concerned" in violation of the Linggadjati Agreement. (c) The republic must have a voice in deciding the future status of Borneo. (d) Dutch New Guinea should be part of East Indonesia. (e) The maintenance of law and order was the sole responsibility of the republic and should not be entrusted to a joint Dutch-Indonesian security force. (f) The republican army should gradually replace the Dutch force. (g) The interim government of the United States of Indonesia should maintain its own diplomatic and consular representation.

(British Prime Min. Clement Attlee Mar. 3 had announced British *de facto* recognition of the Indonesian republican government. The U.S. extended similar recognition Apr. 17.)

Sjarifuddin Replaces Sjahrir as Premier

Sutan Sjahrir resigned as premier of the Indonesian republic June 26, 1947, following ministerial criticism of his policies. Defense Min. Amir Sjarifuddin replaced Sjahrir as premier, and the formation of a new coalition government was announced July 5. In the new cabinet, Sjarifuddin retained his defense ministry portfolio. The new cabinet included 7 members of the Indonesian People's Party (PNL) and 6 Socialists.

Dutch Launch Major Military Drive Against Indonesians

The breakdown of Dutch-Indonesian negotiations signalled the start of a major Dutch military drive against republican positions on Java, Sumatra and Madura July 20, 1947. The Netherlands and republican governments agreed to a cease-fire Aug. 4, but sporadic clashes continued beyond that date. The two sides negotiated the truce after the UN Security Council had called on the Dutch and Indonesians Aug. 1 to halt hostilities.

In explaining the Dutch military action, Netherlands East Indies Gov. van Mook declared in a statement July 20 that the Netherlands government "no longer considers itself bound" by the Oct. 14, 1946 truce pact and the Linggadjati Agreement and "resumes its freedom of action." Van Mook said that months of negotiations with republican officials had shown that they were either unwilling or incapable of carrying out either of these agreements. Citing alleged Indonesian violations of the truce, van Mook said republican soldiers had attacked truce lines, had used "force against people under Dutch protection, and armed action against the Dutch-controlled areas have continued." Van Mook charged that republican authorities continued to hold "hostages," that republican action in the past 2 years had resulted in the uprooting from their homes of "100,000 Indonesians, Chinese and Arabs" and that a republican-imposed food blockade of Medan had "brought part of the population...near famine."

In a broadcast from The Hague July 20, Netherlands Premier Louis Beel said his government had authorized Dutch officials in Indonesia "to take police action...in order to achieve what the republic is incapable of doing." Beel said the Netherlands could no longer tolerate the republic's "daily violations of the Linggadjati Agreement."

The Dutch resumption of military activity in Indonesia was further explained in notes handed to the U.S. and British embassies in The Hague July 20. The messages lauded Sutan Sjahrir for having exerted "a moderate and realistic influence" on Dutch-Indonesian negotiations during his premiership. But the notes asserted that Sjahrir's repudiation and replacement by an irresponsible element in the republican government left the Netherlands government with no hope of fruitful negotiations.

When the Dutch launched their offensive July 20, they encountered little organized opposition from Indonesian republican forces and quickly captured all major republican points in Java, Sumatra and Madura. Republican resistance was confined largely to a "scorched earth" campaign directed principally against the properties of Chinese residents, whom the republicans accused of being pro-Dutch; many estates owned by Europeans and Eurasians also fell victim to the Indonesian scorched-earth policy. Dutch planes carried out widespread raids against airfields in republican-held territory, destroying many of the fields and grounded republican planes. By the time the truce was negotiated Aug. 4, Dutch soldiers had captured all major ports and railways in Java and Sumatra; among the major cities captured in Central Java were Batavia, Cheribon and Malang, the seat of the republican parliament. The Netherlands East Indies government assumed responsibility for internal order in the areas of the 3 islands captured by the Dutch troops.

The Dutch reported Aug. 5 that casualties they had suffered during the July 20-Aug. 4 period totaled 74 killed and 178 wounded. An additional 55 soldiers were killed and 158 wounded in the sporadic clashes with Indonesians that occurred after the Aug. 4 cease-fire, Dutch authorities reported Aug. 20. A Dutch announcement Aug. 27 charged that pro-republican groups and republican troops had committed 500 violations of the cease-fire since Aug. 4.

The Dutch claimed that the Indonesians, in their scorched-earth tactics, had burned down and destroyed many sugar factories in Java and tobacco and rubber plantations in Sumatra, all vital to the country's economy. A Dutch report Aug. 25 said that since the start of the July 20 military operations Indonesians had killed at least 150 Chinese in Java and Sumatra, wounded, and kidnaped hundreds of other Chinese and destroyed many homes of Chinese on those 2 islands.

The Chinese Nationalist Foreign Ministry in Nanking July 29 protested against the attacks on Chinese residents and their properties in Java and Sumatra. The Chinese consul general in Batavia Aug. 7 denied the Indonesian republican charge that the Chinese inhabitants of Java and Sumatra supported the Dutch in their dispute with Indonesia.

UN Arranges Cease-fire, Starts Negotiations

The UN Security Council Aug. 1, 1947 unanimously approved a resolution calling on the Netherlands and republican forces to cease fighting immediately. Both sides complied with the Council's appeal. The Council meeting, called by Australia and India July 22, continued through Aug. 26.

In announcing Dutch acceptance of the truce, NEI Gov. van Mook said in a broadcast from Batavia Aug. 4 that the Netherlands had agreed to the halt in the fighting although it believed that the UN had no right to intervene in the dispute and that the Council's cease-fire resolution constituted interference in the affairs of the Netherlands. The Netherlands' compliance with the resolution was aimed at proving "again that it does not want to neglect any possibility" of bringing an end to "an untenable and lawless situation," van Mook explained.

In a further move to strengthen the cease-fire, the Council Aug. 25 approved by 7-0 vote (4 abstentions: Britain, the USSR, Colombia and Poland) a joint Australian-Chinese Nationalist resolution establishing a UN Consular Commission to implement the Council's truce order. The commission consisted of the 6 foreign consular representatives in Batavia whose countries were represented on the Security Council: the U.S., Britain, Nationalist China, France, Australia and Belgium.

Sporadic violations of the Council's Aug. 1 cease-fire resolution prompted the Council to issue another appeal to both sides Aug. 26. A Polish resolution to that effect was approved by the Council by 10-0 vote (1 abstention: Britain).

The UN Consular Commission, staffed by military officers of the 6 member states, observed the implementation of the cease-fire and established contacts with Netherlands and Indonesian republican authorities. The commission's functions were largely taken over in Sept. 1947 by a 3-nation Committee of Good Offices (CGO) appointed by the Security Council. Its members were representatives of the U.S., Australia and Belgium.

The CGO held its first meeting in Australia Oct. 20, 1947 and then went to Java, where it consulted separately with Netherlands and republican officials. A CGO report filed with the Security Council Nov. 20 stated that "substantial progress" had been made in implementing the UN cease-fire agreement.

Renville Agreement

Indonesian and Netherlands East Indies officials signed a political and truce agreement Jan. 17, 1948 aboard the U.S. naval transport *Renville* in Batavia Bay. Known as the *Renville* Agreement, the pact was worked out in negotiations that had started aboard the vessel Dec. 6, 1947 under the auspices of the UN Committee of Good Offices (CGO). The agreement included 12 Dutch-proposed principles designed to form the basis for further negotiations of a political settlement and a 9-point agreement that provided for a permanent truce to go into effect Jan. 31. The CGO announced Feb. 10 that both sides had carried out the truce agreement. Republican troops had withdrawn from the side of Dutch-held areas; a *status quo* line (known as the "van Mook line") with a demilitarized zone between Dutch and republican positions was established. It was based on positions held by both sides as of Aug. 29, 1947.

The political points of the *Renville* pact were essentially the same as those outlined in the Linggadjati Agreement. They provided for continued Dutch control over the Netherlands East Indies until sovereignty was transferred to the proposed United States of Indonesia (USI). The USI would be an independent state within the Netherlands-Indonesian Union. The Indonesian republic would be a state within the USI. Plebiscites were to be held within 6-12 months to determine whether the inhabitants of Java, Sumatra and Madura wanted their islands to remain part of the republic or to become another state within the USI.

Although the truce section of the *Renville* Agreement was observed, the Dutch-Indonesian dispute remained unresolved as both sides disagreed on implementation of the pact's political proposals.

Renville Agreement Collapses

The UN Committee of Good Offices (CGO) and a Netherlands government ministerial mission negotiated between March and July 1948 in an unsuccessful effort to resolve the political impasse in Indonesia. Failure of the talks was followed by a renewal of large-scale Dutch military action against Indonesian republican forces Dec. 19.

The CGO had renewed its mediation Mar. 15, first holding separate discussions with Dutch officials in Batavia and with Indonesian leaders at Kalioreang, near Jogjakarta. The CGO later held joint meetings with both sides at Kalioreang.

In a report filed with the UN Security Council June 23, the CGO reported no progress and outlined the principal obstacles that blocked Dutch-Indonesian agreement: (1) the technicalities of creating a United States of Indonesia; (2) the Indonesian republic's role in a future Federation of Indonesia; (3) the division of powers between the federation and the proposed Netherlands-Indonesian Union; (4) Indonesian opposition to the prior establishment of an interim federal government and to the Dutch-sponsored *negaras* (states) and *daerahs* (autonomous territories) in Java, Sumatra and Madura. The impasse was further heightened, the CGO pointed out, by the fact that the disputants "evidently consider the *Renville* Agreement as not constituting an agreement in the full sense of the word but simply as a basis for the discussion of a political settlement." The 2 sides were unable to agree as to whether points of the *Renville* Agreement "were to take effect when the parties accepted them, or will become effective when a political agreement has been reached."

Indonesian authorities announced in Jogjakarta July 23 that they had discontinued their negotiations with the Dutch. The announcement said that continued talks would be futile because the Dutch had failed to come up with new suggestions to end a deadlock in effect since June 16 when Netherlands officials had rejected a proposal forwarded by the U.S. and Australian members of the CGO. Indonesian Information Min. Mohammed Natsir announced later July 23 that despite its withdrawal from the talks the republic would continue to observe the truce agreement. Natsir promised that Jogjakarta would resume negotiations if a "new reasonable basis" for such talks was forwarded.

The Netherlands Ministerial Mission, headed by Foreign Min. Dirk U. Stikker, left The Hague for Indonesia Nov. 21. The group conferred in Batavia and Kalioerang with Hatta (who had become Indonesian premier), with delegates of Indonesian states and with the CGO's U.S. member. In a statement made after the mission had left Dec. 5 to return to Holland, Information Min. Natsir announced that the mission had failed to resolve the dispute.

The Netherlands government Dec. 11 filed a report with the CGO on the discussions of the Ministerial Mission in Indonesia. The report said the conferences had shown that "no real cooperation can be expected by the republic in the matter of truce violations, partly because the republican authorities have not been able to enforce their authority on their soldiers." The message noted that in his meetings with Stikker, Premier Hatta had recognized Dutch sovereignty over Indonesia pending a final political solution. But the report said Indonesian officials later rejected the idea of absolute Dutch authority during the interim period. The consequences of this policy, the Netherlands government statement complained, would be that Dutch troops in Indonesia "would gradually have to evacuate the territories now under their control, while the republican forces would remain intact for the time being." In effect, the statement said, this would lead to the creation of 2 armies, and the Netherlands considered that such a situation would be intolerable. Charging that the republic was not honoring the truce and was violating the principles of the *Renville* Agreement, the Dutch statement said the Netherlands could not continue the negotiations and "does not wish to postpone or hinder establishment of the new regime for Indonesia."

The Netherlands repeated its accusations against the Indonesian republic Dec. 18 in a communique in which it formally announced the breaking off of the truce pact.

The Dutch parliament Dec. 21 upheld the Netherlands government's decision to resume fighting in Indonesia. By 80-8 vote Dec. 21 it rejected a Communist-sponsored resolution calling for an immediate cease-fire. Premier Willem Drees charged in parliamentary debate that since July the Indonesian republic had violated the *Renville* Agreement by sending thousands of soldiers into Netherlands-controlled territory from which they had withdrawn under terms of the agreement. The troops' purpose, Drees said, was "to disturb law and order and. . .to exercise terrorism over Indonesian officials."

A CGO report filed with the UN Security Council Dec. 20 had stated that the Netherlands had violated the *Renville* Agreement by failing to give advance notice of its intentions to end the truce.

Premier Sjarifuddin Forced to Resign

Premier Amir Sjarifuddin, who had signed the *Renville* Agreement as head of the republican delegation, was accused by extremist Indonesian nationalists of having bowed to Dutch demands to reach a settlement. The mounting criticism forced Sjarifuddin to resign Jan. 23, 1948. Pres. Sukarno appointed Vice Pres. Mohammad Hatta as premier. Hatta formed a new cabinet Jan. 31. In it he held the additional post of defense minister. The cabinet, including most of the members of the Sjarifuddin government, consisted largely of members of the Moslem Masjumi Party and the National Party (PNI); all Socialists and leftwingers were barred.

Interim Federal Government Established

An interim federal government was established in Batavia Jan. 13, 1948. The regime included Dutch and Indonesian representatives of the Netherlands East Indies government and of the non-republican territories. It was intended as a preliminary step toward the setting up of the projected United States of Indonesia. NEI Gov. van Mook was named president of the federal government and Raden Abdulkadir Widjojoamodjo was chosen deputy lieutenant governor-general.

The territory under control of the interim regime comprised the *negaras* (states) and *daerahs* (autonomous territories), which the Dutch had helped create in 1947. The federal government's jurisdiction expanded as new *negaras* and *daerahs* came into existence by the end of 1948. Territorial composition of the federal government: *negaras* — East Indonesia (Celebes, Bali, Lombok, Sumba, Sumbawa, Flores, Halmahera, Timor and the Moluccas), East Sumatra, Madura, West Java, South Sumatra and East Java; *daerahs* — Borneo (5), Banka and Billiton.

The Indonesian republic had recognized the *negara* of East Indonesia. But it had expressed opposition to the establishment of the *negaras* on its territories of Java, Sumatra and Madura. In protests to the UN Good Offices Committee, the republic had charged that the Dutch had encouraged the creation of the *negaras* in order to weaken the republic. The protests also had contended that the *negaras* were in violation of the Linggidjati Agreement, which had given the republic *de facto* authority over Java, Sumatra and Madura.

The resignation of van Mook as governor general of the Netherlands East Indies was announced Oct. 14, 1948. Van Mook was succeeded by Louis Beel, who had been replaced as premier of the Netherlands by Willem Drees following general elections in July. Beel was sworn in by Queen Juliana Oct. 31 as High Commissioner for the Crown in Indonesia, a new post approved by the Dutch parliament Oct. 26-29. The position of governor general was abolished. Parliament also formally renamed the Netherlands East Indies as Indonesia.

Beel arrived in Batavia Nov. 3 to assume his new duties.

Dutch Renew Military Attacks; UN Arranges Truce

Dutch troops launched an all-out military drive against Indonesian republican forces in Java and Sumatra Dec. 19, 1948, a day after the Netherlands government had announced that it would no longer honor the truce agreement. As in previous flare-ups of fighting, the UN intervened and worked out a truce pact in 1949. The cease-fire was followed by a definitive political solution, negotiated in Nov. 1949, under which the Netherlands transferred full political sovereignty to a United States of Indonesia.

The Dutch attack was greeted with widespread international condemnation. The U.S. reacted Dec. 22 by suspending Marshall Plan aid to the Netherlands East Indies. But a Dutch spokesman in New York insisted Dec. 23 that his country's "police action" was a blow against Indonesian Communists who, he said, had infiltrated the republican army and planned to use it in an uprising Jan. 1.

In the Java-Sumatra fighting, Indonesian soldiers offered little resistance as superior numbers of Dutch ground troops, paratroops and marines penetrated the "van Mook line" on both islands. Part of the Dutch force made amphibious landings on Java and Sumatra. The Dutch reported the capture of Jogjakarta during the first day's fighting. The port of Rembang was taken Dec. 21. The Sumatran capital of Bukittinggi was captured the following day. Java was reported under Dutch control Dec. 31, and all major fighting there was said to have ended Jan. 2, 1949, except for mopping-up operations. The Dutch reported cessation of hostilities on Sumatra Jan. 5. Gen. Simon H. Spoor, head of Dutch military forces, reported Jan. 2 that Dutch casualties through Dec. 19 had totaled 66 killed and 172 wounded.

Although Dutch authorities boasted of total military success, a UN Committee of Good Offices (CGO) report issued Jan. 14 indicated that Indonesian forces were continuing to resist on

Java. The CGO statement said Indonesian guerrillas were particularly active in the Madioen and Kediri sectors of Central Java, blowing up roads and bridges and pinning down hundreds of Dutch troops.

At the outset of the fighing Dec. 19, republican leaders, including Pres. Sukarno and Premier Hatta, had been arrested in Jogjakarta. They were later transferred to Banka, an island off Sumatra. The republican leaders were released from detention but confined to Banka. Sukarno, Hatta and the others were finally returned to Jogjakarta June 29, 1949 under a UN-sponsored Dutch-Indonesian military agreement.

The UN Security Council held hearings in Paris Dec. 22-31, 1948 to consider the new crisis resulting from Dutch rejection of the truce agreement and the military clashes that followed. Council intervention had been requested by the U.S., Australia and the UN CGO.

The Council, at the Dec. 24 meeting, approved by 7-0 vote (4 abstentions) a resolution urging: (a) an immediate cease-fire by Dutch and Indonesian forces; (b) Dutch release of Sukarno and other Indonesian republican leaders on Banka. Voting for the resolution: the U.S., Britain, Nationalist China, Canada, Argentina, Colombia and Syria; abstaining: the Soviet Union, France, Belgium and Ukraine.

During a resumption of debate Jan. 7, 1949, Indonesian delegate L. M. Palar charged that the Netherlands continued to defy the Council's Dec. 24 resolution by failing to comply with the cease-fire order and by refusing to release the imprisoned republican officials. Netherlands delegate Jan H. van Roijen had disclosed earlier that Sukarno, Hatta and the other government officials had been released from house arrest but remained confined to Banka.

The Security Council's hearings on Indonesia shifted to the UN's temporary headquarters at Lake Success, N.Y. Jan. 21. After a week of debate, the Council Jan. 28 adopted a resolution calling on the Netherlands to establish the promised interim federal government in Indonesia by Mar. 15, 1949 and to transfer sovereignty to the United States of Indonesia (one of the proposed members of the federal system) by July 1, 1950. The Council urged immediate Dutch-Indonesian negotiations to achieve those political goals. The resolution repeated previous Council calls for an immediate halt in military operations and for the release by the Dutch of Indonesian political prisoners.

Under the resolution, the CGO in Batavia was renamed the UN Commission for Indonesia (UNCI) and was empowered to continue to represent the Security Council in Indonesia.

The Netherlands government responded to the Council's Jan. 28 resolution by announcing Feb. 27 that it would "endeavor to effect the transfer of sovereignty considerably earlier than July 1, 1950." The statement, issued simultaneously in The Hague and in Batavia, said the Dutch were ready to comply with other aspects of the Council's resolution, including the release of imprisoned republican leaders. The statement further proposed a Dutch-Indonesian round-table conference in The Hague Mar. 12 to discuss the proposed transfer of sovereignty.

The Dutch suggestion for a round-table conference was rejected Feb. 28 by Mohammed Rum, chairman of the republican delegation to the UNCI (UN Commission for Indonesia). He said the proposal "cuts across and explicitly rejects" the Security Council's Jan. 28 resolution. The Dutch proposal was similarly criticized by UNCI in a report filed with the Security Council Mar. 2.

To deal with the latest impasse, the Security Council reconvened Mar. 10-13 and met again Mar. 23. On the latter date the Council approved by 8-0 vote (3 abstentions: the Soviet Union, Ukraine and France) a Canadian resolution calling on UNCI (a) to arrange an immediate preliminary Dutch-republican conference and (b) to implement the Council's previous resolutions relating to a truce, the return of the republican government to Jogjakarta and the release of republican political prisoners held by Dutch forces.

The Council's resolution led to a preliminary conference held in Batavia under UNCI auspices Apr. 15-May 7, 1949. The meeting was attended by Dutch and republican representatives and by delegations of the non-republican territories of Indonesia. The Netherlands agreed at the talks to permit the republican government to return to Jogjakarta, to halt military operations immediately and to release all prisoners seized since Dec. 17, 1948. The Dutch also pledged not to establish or recognize *negaras* or *daerahs* in territories that had been under republican control prior to Dec. 19, 1948.

The republican delegation agreed at the Batavia conference to cease guerrilla activities against Dutch forces and to participate in the proposed round-table conference once the republican government was permitted to return to Jogjakarta.

In compliance with the UN Security Council's resolution, Dutch forces evacuated Jogjakarta June 24-29 and were replaced by republican troops. On completion of the Dutch evacuation, Pres. Sukarno, Premier Hatta and other republican leaders were released from Banka and flown to Jogjakarta, where they reestablished their government after a 6-month hiatus.

A further conference in Batavia between Dutch and republican representatives under UNCI auspices July 25-29 led to a cease-fire agreement. Hostilities were halted in Java Aug. 10-11 and in Sumatra Aug. 14-15.

A joint Dutch-Indonesian proclamation issued Aug. 3 had said: (a) All political prisoners and war captives would be released immediately. (b) Dutch and republican forces would remain in areas under their control. (c) 13 cease-fire committees of Dutch and Indonesian representatives would be established to patrol zones in Java and Sumatra for passage of civilians and goods other than arms and ammunition; the committees would be under the supervision of a board of UN military advisers.

UNCI formally reported to the UN Security Council Aug. 12 that the republican government had been reestablished in Jogjakarta, that a cease-fire had gone into effect and that Dutch and republican officials had agreed to meet at a round-table conference in The Hague to negotiate a final political settlement. The report said the Council's objectives in Indonesia had thus been achieved, and it expressed hope for "the beginning of a new era for the peoples of the Netherlands and Indonesia."

Communist Revolt Suppressed

The Indonesian republic faced its first internal threat Sept. 19, 1948 when a Communist revolt broke out at Madioen, Java, 35 miles northeast of Jogjakarta. Republican forces went into action against the rebels, and Pres. Sukarno announced

Oct. 17 that the uprising had been suppressed, except for mopping-up operations.

The revolt was led by Indonesian Communist Party leader Muso, who had returned to Java Aug. 12 after spending 23 years in Moscow. The armed Communists, assisted by a dissident brigade of the Indonesian army, captured Madioen, and Muso proclaimed a "soviet republic" in the city of 100,000. Sukarno declared a state of martial law throughout the republic and denounced the Communists as "traitors."

Parliament Sept. 20 granted Sukarno unlimited powers for 3 months to cope with the emergency and banned all leftwing organizations. Several hundred Communists were arrested in Jogjakarta Sept. 20, and all Communist centers in the city were shut.

The Indonesian army launched a drive Sept. 23 against the rebels in Madioen and in 3 smaller towns nearby and captured all the Communist strongholds Sept. 30. Muso fled but was reported killed Oct. 31 in a clash with republican forces near Sumanding. Muso's 2d-in-command, Alimin, was reported Nov. 4 to have been executed following his capture at Madioen. Alimin had led the Indonesian Communist Party (*Partai Kommunis Indonesia*, or PKI) while Muso was in Moscow. Also seized in Madioen (reported Nov. 30) was ex-Premier Amir Sjarifuddin. Sjarifuddin had been sought following his announcement Aug. 31 that the Indonesian Republic Socialist Party, which he headed, had merged with the PKI. Sjarifuddin had disclosed at the time that he had been a secret Communist Party member since 1935.

The PKI's increasing activities had prompted Dutch authorities Sept. 15, 1948 to outlaw the party in Netherlands East Indies territories.

Netherlands Ends Its Rule of Indonesia

The Netherlands government Dec. 27, 1949 formally conferred sovereignty on the United States of Indonesia (USI) as an independent country. The ceremonies, held in Amsterdam, marked the end of 350 years of Dutch rule in the East Indies. The transfer of sovereignty had been negotiated at a round-table conference held at The Hague Aug. 23-Nov. 2. The 10-week meeting was attended by about 120 delegates of the

Netherlands government, the Indonesian republic, the non-republican federal areas (*negaras and daerahs*) and the UN Commission for Indonesia.

Major provisions of the final agreement, signed Nov. 2 by Netherlands, republican and federal officials:

■ The USI was to be given its independence no later than Dec. 30, 1949. It was to comprise the Indonesian republic and the 15 federal states that had been created under Dutch auspices. The federal areas included 5 Borneo states, 5 *negaras* and *daerahs* on the islands of Sumatra and Java and several smaller islands.

■ A Statute of the Netherlands-Indonesian Union provided for a loose partnership of the USI and the Netherlands under which the 2 states would cooperate in such areas as defense, foreign relations, economy, finance and cultural matters. A Union Court of Arbitration would settle future Dutch-Indonesian disputes. The USI recognized Dutch Queen Juliana as symbolic head of the union.

■ Dutch troops were to withdraw from Indonesia within 6 months after the transfer of sovereignty: The Dutch navy was to pull out of Indonesian waters in a year.

■ The USI promised to protect Dutch investments and recognized the huge Dutch commercial interest in Indonesia.

The conference had failed to resolve the question of Dutch New Guinea. The Netherlands resisted Indonesian demands that the territory become part of the USI. Because of this impasse, it was agreed that Dutch New Guinea would remain under Netherlands control for a year pending further Dutch-Indonesian negotiation of the dispute.

A provisional constitution for the USI had been signed at The Hague round-table conference Oct. 30. It embodied the constitutional proposals that had been adopted at an Inter-Indonesian Conference in Jogjakarta July 20-Aug. 2, 1949, preparatory to the round-table conference. The Jogjakarta meeting was attended by republican and federal delegates. The provisional charter outlined the structural composition of the USI and contained these other proposals: (a) A 150-member People's Assembly (lower house) and a Senate (upper house) would be established. The Assembly would have 50 republican and 100 federal members; it would have full legislative powers. The Senate would be made up of 2 members from each territory and have advisory powers. The People's Assembly, which would replace the People's Representative Assembly, would be chosen in a democratic election one year after the transfer of sovereignty. Soon after the establishment of the People's Assembly, a Constituent Assembly would be formed to draw up a permanent constitution. (b) The president of the USI would be the constitutional head of government and would appoint a premier. (c) USI citizenship would be open to all Indonesians who had been subjects of the Netherlands or of the former republic. All Chinese, Arabs and Europeans in Indonesia would have the choice of becoming USI citizens.

The 2 houses of the Dutch parliament approved The Hague agreements Dec. 9 and 21. The Indonesian republican parliament approved the pact Dec. 14 by 226-62 vote (31 abstentions). The negative votes were cast by 52 members of the Indonesian Communist Party and 10 independents. Representatives of all *negaras* and *daerahs* approved the provisional constitution at a meeting in Batavia Dec. 14.

The Hague Dec. 14 announced the appointment of Dr. Hans M. Hirschfeld as the first Netherlands High Commissioner to Indonesia, as provided for by the Union Statute. He assumed his duties in Indonesia Dec. 28. (Louis Beel had resigned as Netherlands representative to Indonesia May 10 after disagreeing with government policy. He had been replaced by A. H. J. Lovink May 19.)

One day after the signing of The Hague agreements, Dutch authorities began to implement the military provisions of the pact. Dutch officials Nov. 3 announced the immediate release of thousands of Indonesian political prisoners. Dutch troops evacuated Surakarta, Java Nov. 14. Dutch forces started to turn over control of Batavia and Surabaya to Indonesian troops Dec. 10.

Sukarno Heads U.S. of Indonesia

Sukarno, president of the Indonesian republic since 1945, was elected first president of the United States of Indonesia

Dec. 16, 1949. He was chosen unanimously by representatives of all *negaras* and *daerahs* at a meeting in Jogjakarta. Sukarno took the oath of office Dec. 17.

Mohammed Hatta, premier of the Indonesian republic since 1948, was chosen as premier of the USI by Sukarno Dec. 18. Hatta announced the formation of a 16-member cabinet Dec. 20. 11 ministers were republicans, 5 ministers were from the federalist territories. Hatta temporarily held the post of foreign minister.

The cabinet: *Republican members*: Premier & Foreign — Hatta; Defense — Sultan (of Jogjakarta) Hamengku Buwono; Economic Affairs — Djuanda; Finance — Sjafruddin Prawiranegara; Justice — Supomo; Labor — Wilopo; Health — Johannes Leimena; Transport & Waterways — H. Loah; Education — Abu Hanifah; Religious Affairs — Wahid Hasjim; Minister Without Portfolio — Mohammed Rum. *Federalist members:* Home Affairs — Anak Agung Gde Agung; Social Affairs — Purwanegara; Information — Arnold Mononutu; Ministers Without Portfolio — Hamid Alkadrie, Suparmo.

Ceremonies were held Dec. 27 in Batavia, seat of the former Dutch colonial rulers, as the USI was granted its independence. The Dutch flag was lowered and the Indonesian flag was raised. The city became the capital of the USI and reverted to its ancient Indonesian name of Jakarta, meaning important city.

Sukarno arrived in Jakarta Dec. 28 to establish the USI government there. He declared: "We are now on peaceful terms with the Dutch and other foreigners. They are our guests. Show hospitality to them."

The U.S. and other countries extended immediate recognition to the new Indonesian government.

1950-56

The United States of Indonesia (USI) became a unified nation with a strong central government Aug. 15, 1950, after republican and federal representatives agreed to the merger July 20. The unification, however, was challenged almost immediately by armed separatists who unsuccessfully sought autonomy for various parts of Indonesia.

Following unification the country's name was formally changed to Republic of Indonesia. Its territory included all the islands of Indonesia, except Dutch New Guinea, whose disposition at that time was still subject to Dutch-Indonesian negotiation. Republican Pres. Sukarno became president of the unitary state, and Jakarta remained the national capital.

A constitution containing the essential elements of the former republican charter was adopted by the USI parliament before it was dissolved. The constitution provided for a single-house legislature—the House of Representatives. The House was made up of members of the former USI (federal) and Indonesian republic parliaments. Communist deputies boycotted the meetings in which the new unified state was approved. South Molucca, in revolt since Apr. 26, also refused to recognize the new constitution.

The drive for territorial and political unity had started earlier in 1950 when the Dutch-sponsored *negaras* and *daerahs* agreed to join the republic. A decree signed by Sukarno Mar. 9 brought the *negaras* of East Java, Central Java and the Sumatran town of Padang under republican rule. Another decree signed by Sukarno Mar. 12 merged the *negara* of West Java with the republic. The West Java legislature had voted to dissolve the *negara* Jan. 31 and to join the USI for protection against a revolt that had broken out there Jan. 23. The *daerah* of South Celebes agreed Apr. 26 to join the republic, and the ruling councils of the *daerahs* of North Celebes and Minhassa approved a similar move Apr. 30. The drive for unity was further strengthened by an announcement May 9 that the governments of the *negaras* of East Indonesia and East Sumatra had agreed to the formation of a united Indonesian republic.

The Netherlands government sent to the UN Indonesian Commission May 15 a note expressing concern that the absorption of the *negaras* into the republic had abridged the rights of the *negaras* to self-government. In a separate message to the USI government, the Dutch regime questioned whether the rights of the *negaras* would be protected in a future unitary state.

Indonesia's admission as the 60th member of the UN was unanimously approved by the UN Security Council Sept. 26, 1950 and by the General Assembly Sept. 28.

Uprisings in West Java & East Indonesia

Armed revolts broke out in West Java and East Indonesia during 1950 in opposition to the move to form a unitary state. The unrest was heightened by the opposition of Indonesian soldiers of the Netherlands Indies army to a Dutch-Indonesian proposal to merge part of that force with the Indonesian army.

The West Java revolt was led by Capt. Raymond P. P. Westerling, a Dutch citizen of Turkish descent and a Moslem. After being demobilized from the Dutch forces, Westerling formed a rebel group called the "Army of the Heavenly Host," which comprised dissident Indonesians, Eurasians and Europeans. Westerling's objectives were outlined in an ultimatum handed to the USI and West Javanese governments Jan. 10, 1950. Westerling announced that his rebel group was determined to maintain the autonomy of West Java. He insisted that his force be recognized as West Java's official army because, he claimed, the central government's troops were incapable of maintaining order there. Westerling warned the USI and West Javanese regimes that unless he received a positive reply by Jan. 12, he "might be unable to control" the men under his command.

Westerling's forces began their armed uprising Jan. 23 after the ultimatum was ignored. The rebels first captured Tjimahi, 7 miles west of Bandung. After being joined by about 300 deserters from the Netherlands Indies and West Javanese armies, they attacked Bandung and forced government troops to abandon the southern part of the city. The insurgents withdrew later Jan. 23 when loyal Netherlands Indies troops intervened, but Westerling's soldiers carried out raids against 2 cities in the Bandung area.

The West Java revolt collapsed Jan. 26 with an unsuccessful rebel assault on Jakarta. A force of about 100 rebels managed to penetrate the city's defenses, but they quickly surrendered to government troops. Another 2,000 rebels headed for Jakarta, but they too gave up after being intercepted by USI troops outside the city.

Westerling fled to Singapore Feb. 22 to escape arrest under a warrant that had been issued by the USI government Jan. 24. Singapore authorities seized Westerling and deported him Aug. 22 after rejecting a USI government request Aug. 8 for his extradition. Westerling arrived in Belgium and was granted political asylum there Aug. 24.

The USI government, meanwhile, cracked down on other leaders of the West Javanese revolt. West Javanese Premier Anwar Tjokroaminoto was arrested Jan. 24 on charges of conspiring with Westerling and the Darul Islam, a Moslem guerrilla movement, in a plot to establish a West Javanese Islamic state. Sultan Abdul Hamid, a minister without portfolio in the USI government, was arrested Apr. 5 on charges of being "one of the prime movers" in the revolt. A Dutch court-martial in Jakarta July 14 jailed 123 Indonesian soldiers of the Netherlands army who had joined the rebels. They received prison terms ranging from 10 months to a year.

The East Indonesian uprising took the form of 2 separate and uncoordinated revolts—in Macassar (on the island of Celebes), capital of the state, and in a group of islands east of Celebes—Ceram, Amboina, Buru and Banda—known as the South Moluccas.

Rebel forces seized Macassar Apr. 5 and forced the USI army garrison there to surrender. The insurgents were members of a former Netherlands Indies army company that had been incorporated into the government army a few days earlier. East Indonesian State police and Netherlands Indies troops also joined the rebels. Capt. Abdul Aziz, leader of the uprising, said the dissidents had acted to prevent the landing in Macassar earlier Apr. 5 of 900 former republican troops who had arrived from Java by ship. Aziz charged that the troops, who had been refused permission to disembark, had planned "to liquidate systematically the East Indonesian State." A force of 2,000 USI troops were sent to Macassar Apr. 19 after the rebels had defied repeated government ultimatums to surrender. The insurgents surrendered the city without resistance after the USI troops moved in. Aziz, who had flown to Jakarta Apr. 14 to discuss the situation with USI officials, was arrested on his arrival.

Netherland Indies army troops on Amboina mutinied Apr. 26 and declared an independent "Republic of the South Moluccas." The rebels asserted that East Indonesia was no longer able to guarantee "the maintenance of its position as an autonomous state of the USI." The USI did not react to the rebellion until May 31, when it announced that Amboina had been sealed off by a naval blockade in preparation for military action.

The USI landed troops on the island of Buru July 14 and on Ceram July 21-23. The USI claimed that little resistance was encountered in either operation. The main rebel resistance was centered on Amboina, where the heaviest fighting of the South Molucca uprising was to follow.

After massing a large land, sea and air force, the USI landed troops on Amboina Sept. 28. The USI troops struck in the north of the island and fought their way to the town of Amboina Oct. 6, encountering heavy resistance. Amboina fell to Indonesian troops Nov. 3 after it had been heavily pounded by warships and planes. Of the 20,000 USI troops involved in the Amboina operation, 4,000 were killed or wounded. About 500 of the 1,000 Ambonese rebels were reported to be casualties. 80% of the buildings in the town of Amboina were destroyed and about 5,000 civilians were killed or injured in the fighting. Capt. Abdul Aziz, leader of the Macassar revolt, was sentenced to 14 years in prison by a military court in Jogjakarta

Apr. 8, 1953. The Indonesian Supreme Court the same day gave Sultan Abdul Hamid a 10-year prison sentence for involvement in the West Javanese uprising. Hamid, whose trial had started Feb. 25, had pleaded not guilty to charges of participating in the uprising. But he confessed that he had sought to interest Capt. Westerling in a plot to arrest Indonesian cabinet ministers, to execute the defense minister and the army chief of staff and then to ask Pres. Sukarno to permit Hamid to form a new government with Hamid as defense minister.

Political Background to Revolts

The Indonesian government had suppressed the South Moluccan revolt with force despite appeals by the UN Indonesian Commission for a peaceful solution of the dispute. The Indonesian military action also gave emphasis to the remaining unresolved differences between Dutch and Indonesian authorities.

The UN Indonesian Commission proposed to the Indonesian government Aug. 4 and Sept. 25, 1950 that the commission be permitted to visit Amboina to persuade the rebels to negotiate with Jakarta. The Indonesian government rejected the proposals on the ground that commission intervention "would constitute encouragement to the Ambonese rebels." The commission again appealed to Indonesia Oct. 6, this time at the behest of the Netherlands government. The commission's message, issued while fighting was in progress on Amboina, suggested that Indonesia suspend all military action and allow the commission to mediate. An Indonesian government reply Oct. 10 rejected the commission's plea and charged that the uprising had resulted from Netherlands failure to maintain discipline among the Ambonese troops of the Netherlands Indies army.

Netherlands sympathy with the Ambonese rebels was evidenced by the presence in The Hague of representatives of the "South Moluccan Republic." These representatives announced Oct. 5 that they had appealed to the UN Indonesian Commission, British Prime Min. Clement Attlee and U.S. Pres. Harry S. Truman to intervene.

Netherlands Premier Willem Drees Oct. 3, in a note to Indonesian Premier Mohammed Natsir, expressed "shock" over the Indonesian military action. Natsir, replying Oct. 4, reminded Drees that the Netherlands was responsible for the Ambonese troops in its military forces; he said The Hague should have disciplined the Ambonese troops when they rebelled.

The Indonesian parliament Oct. 9 adopted a resolution assailing Drees' message to Natsir as "outside intervention in the affairs of Indonesia."

Pres. Sukarno had asserted in a broadcast Oct. 5 that Dutch action in regard to Indonesian soldiers of the Netherlands Indies army was responsible for the unrest that had gripped Indonesia since the 1949 sovereignty transfer agreements. Sukarno charged that the West Javanese and East Indonesian revolts had resulted from the failure of Dutch officers to properly implement the military arrangements of those agreements.

Netherlands Indies Army Disbanded

The Netherlands Indies army and the Netherlands army command in Indonesia were formally dissolved July 26, 1950. The command's headquarters in Jakarta had been handed over to the Indonesian army July 25.

Dutch and Indonesian authorities had agreed on the dissolution action and had announced it in a joint communiqué May 9. According to the communiqué, 15,000 Netherlands Indies army troops had been transferred to the Indonesian armed forces, and 20,000 Dutch and Eurasian soldiers were being repatriated to Holland.

A supplemental Dutch-Indonesian agreement July 14 established a "resettlement command," under supervision of the Netherlands High Commissioner's Office, to provide for the resettlement and repatriation of Dutch soldiers and Indonesian members of the Netherlands Indies army. The accord provided for turning over the Netherlands Indies army equipment to the Indonesian armed forces.

The Netherlands military mission in Indonesia was officially terminated Dec. 16, 1953.

Cabinet Changes

Mohammed Natsir was replaced as premier by Sukiman Wirjosandjojo Apr. 26, 1951. Sukiman, leader of the Masjumi (Moslem) party, resigned as premier Feb. 23, 1952 in a dispute involving the issue of American aid. Sukiman withdrew after it was learned that Foreign Min. Achmed Subardjo, a Nationalist Party member, had secretly agreed to accept U.S. Mutual Security funds. Proposed acceptance of American economic assistance had been rejected by the Masjumi party Feb. 13 and by the Nationalist Party Feb. 16.

Sukiman remained in a caretaker position until he was replaced as premier Apr. 1 by Dr. Wilopo. Wilopo, a member of the Nationalist Party, opposed U.S. aid. In the new cabinet he formed, Wilopo held the additional position of acting foreign minister.

Despite Wilopo's opposition to American aid, the Indonesian government May 17 agreed to accept U.S. technical and economic assistance — but not military aid — under the U.S. Mutual Security program.

Government Resists Army Intervention

The stability of the Indonesian government was further threatened in 1952 by efforts of dissident army elements to intervene in the country's political affairs. The government successfully resisted these attempts as it received strong political support and the backing of pro-government army elements who carried out a series of mutinies against the army's anti-government wing.

Widespread unrest in the army centered on opposition to the policies of the defense minister, the Sultan of Jogjakarta, Hamengku Buwono I, and the Army High Command. Both had proposed reducing army strength from 200,000 men to 100,000. The sultan and the High Command also were criticized for allegedly favoring Indonesians in the former Netherlands Indies army over Indonesian Nationalist soldiers who had fought against the Dutch in the war of independence. The Defense Ministry also was criticized for cooperating too closely with the Netherlands military mission.

In the wake of these criticisms, the Indonesian parliament Oct. 16, 1952 approved a motion to investigate the Defense Ministry. This parliamentary action precipitated a violent demonstration in Jakarta the following day. 5,000 persons marched through the streets demanding the dissolution of parliament. The mob later forced its way into the parliament building. The demonstrators finally left after Pres. Sukarno assured them in an address that elections would be held "after the revolution had been completed by the incorporation of West Irian [Dutch New Guinea] in Indonesia." Sukarno adjourned parliament Oct. 19.

Premier Wilopo charged Oct. 21 that the purpose of the Jakarta demonstration was "to check the authority of parliament and bring about a situation in which the government would no longer be able to function."

A government statement issued Nov. 22 confirmed reports that the army had played a leading role in the Jakarta demonstrations. According to the statement, army officers had organized the rally, had aimed artillery at the parliament building and presidential palace and had arrested several members of parliament. The government said the army dissidents had urged Sukarno Oct. 17 to dissolve parliament and convene a new parliament as soon as possible. The government assailed these demands as "interference in the political field." It warned that the Jakarta regime would not tolerate "these transgressions of the bounds of the army's task."

The government Nov. 26 charged that Col. Abdul Haris Nasution, army chief of staff, and other high-ranking officers were primarily responsible for the Jakarta disturbances.

Pro-government army officers carried out 3 separate mutinies against divisional commanders supporting the sultan of Jogjakarta. 3 of the Indonesian army's 7 divisions were involved. In the first action, Oct. 24, a group of officers led by Lt. Col. Sudirman seized control of the 5th Division, based at Surabaya, East Java. The deposed acting divisional commander, Lt. Col. Sunwondho, was accused of supporting the Jakarta demonstrations. In the 2d mutiny, at Macassar Nov. 15, 7th Division officers ousted the commander, Col. Subroto, and elevated Col. Warouw to the post. Sudirman and Warouw both pledged loyalty to Pres. Sukarno. The 3d mutiny was carried out Nov. 23 by officers of the 2d Division, based at Palembang, South Sumatra. The divisional commander, Lt. Col. Kosasih, was ousted and replaced by Lt. Col. Kretarto. Under a compromise agreement reached by the division's opposing factions Nov. 26, Kretarto agreed to resign in favor of Col. Utojo, appointed by the government.

The government's stand against the army dissidents was further strengthened Nov. 15 when representatives of all political parties (except Socialists) met in Palembang and issued a declaration urging the recall of parliament and demanding action against "groups who seek to destroy democracy in Indonesia." A Nationalist Party conference Dec. 11 approved a resolution expressing support for the government in its struggle with the army.

Encouraged by the strong support it had received in political and army ranks, the government Dec. 5 dismissed Col. Nasution as army chief of staff. Col. Bambang Sugeng was appointed acting chief of staff Dec. 17.

The sultan of Jogjakarta resigned as defense minister Jan. 2, 1953 in protest against Sugeng's decision to allow Lt. Col. Warouw to remain as commander of the 7th Division. Deputy Premier Mangkusasmito temporarily assumed control of the Defense Ministry Jan. 3.

Sastroamidjojo Replaces Wilopo

Premier Wilopo and his cabinet resigned June 3, 1953 in a dispute between the 2 principal parties of his coalition government—the Nationalists and the Masjumi (Moslem) party. A new 10-party coalition cabinet was formed July 30 with Dr. Ali Sastroamidjojo of the Nationalists as premier.

The issues that led to the resignation of Wilopo's cabinet were Nationalist opposition to the government's agrarian policy and Masjumi refusal to accept Nationalist demands for the nationalization of the Royal Dutch-Shell Co.'s oilfields in North Sumatra.

Nationalist-Masjumi differences prevented the 2 parties from agreeing on the formation of a new cabinet. As a result, the task was handed over July 20 to Wongsonegoro, chairman of the Greater Indonesian Federation. Wongsonegoro July 30 announced the formation of the new cabinet, to which he was appointed first vice premier.

Former coalition parties, including the Masjumi and the Socialist, Christian and Catholic parties, were not represented in Sastroamidjojo's cabinet. The exclusion of the Masjumi (for the first time since 1949) and the Socialists followed charges levelled against them during negotiations to replace Wilopo's government. Masjumi was accused of having provided a legal "cover" for the Darul Islam movement, which sought to overthrow the republic and establish an Islamic state. Darul Islam had stepped up its terrorist activity in West Java as a prelude to a full-scale uprising that eventually broke out Sept. 20 in North Sumatra. The Socialist Party was barred from the Sastroamidjojo cabinet for alleged complicity in the army-supported anti-government riots in Jakarta Oct. 17, 1952.

The alleged growing menace of Darul Islam was stressed in an address by Premier Sastroamidjojo in parliament Aug. 25. Outlining government policy, Sastroamidjojo warned that military measures would be taken against Darul Islam or any other terrorist group that sought to subvert the Indonesian regime.

Sastroamidjojo's cabinet received a vote of confidence in parliament Sept. 10.

Darul Islam Revolt Crushed

Armed followers of the Darul Islam movement began their full-scale revolt in the Atjeh sub-district of North Sumatra Sept. 20, 1953. The insurgents attacked army and police barracks in towns on the east coast between Kutaradja and Medan. Some of the heaviest fighting occurred Sept. 20-26 at Lhoseumawe, where about 100 rebels were killed in clashes with government troops and police. Government sources Oct. 3 reported the recapture of several towns in North Sumatra. Another major action was carried out by the Moslem rebels in the Meureudoe area Oct. 14. Attacking with mortars and automatic weapons, the insurgents forced government army and police units to retreat to the coast after 13 hours of fierce fighting. Sporadic clashes continued thereafter throughout the Atjeh district, and the government forces generally kept the upper hand. Final rebel resistance was crushed Nov. 23 when government forces recaptured Takengon, the last insurgent stronghold.

The Darul Islam uprising was led by Daud Beureuh, chairman of the Moslem Association of Religious Teachers of Atjeh (PUSA). PUSA had seized power in Atjeh in 1945 after the Japanese capitulation. The district was declared a separate province with Daud Beureuh as governor. Atjeh was later absorbed into the province of North Sumatra. This precipitated Darul Islam's campaign against the Central and North Sumatra provincial governments, culminating in the Sept. 20 revolt.

Premier Sastroamidjojo Resigns

Premier Sastroamidjojo and his cabinet, in office since July 30, 1953, resigned July 24, 1955. The resignation followed a dispute between the government and dissident army leaders.

The government June 26 had appointed Col. Utojo, commander in South Sumatra, to replace Maj. Gen. Sugeng as chief of staff. Sugeng had quit for reasons of health. A majority of senior army officers, led by Lt. Col. Zulkifi Lubis, deputy chief of staff, came out against Utojo's appointment on the ground that it had been made for political reasons. The army officers also charged that Utojo was not qualified for the post.

The government rejected the officers' protest. This led to a refusal by the dissident military leaders to recognize Utojo's authority. Lubis was suspended June 28 as deputy chief of staff on a charge of insubordination. The government and army dissidents held a series of conferences to resolve the dispute. The talks, however, were fruitless, and the Sastroamidjojo government stepped down July 24.

A new government was formed Aug. 11 with Burhanuddin Harahap, 38, heading it as premier and defense minister. Harahap was a member of the Masjumi party's executive. Djanu Ismadi, of the Indonesian People's Party, was named first vice premier.

In a move to placate the dissident army officers, Harahap's government Aug. 16 accepted the resignation of Col. Utojo and reinstated Col. Lubis as acting chief of staff.

Parliamentary Elections

The first general elections for Indonesia's 260-member House of Representatives was held Sept. 29-Nov. 30, 1955. 168 parties entered candidates. Although no single party obtained a majority, pro-government parties held a total of 189 seats. According to final results announced Mar. 1, 1956: The Masjumi and Nationalist parties received 57 seats each. The Nahdlatul-'Ulama (Moslem association) won 45 seats, the Communist Party 39. The remaining seats were divided among 24 smaller parties.

Following the election of a new House of Representatives, Premier Harahap handed in his resignation Mar. 3, 1956. Pres. Sukarno called on ex-Premier Ali Sastroamidjojo to form a new government with the broadest possible base. Sastroamidjojo appointed a coalition cabinet comprised of Indonesia's major parties—the Nationalists, the Masjumi, the Nahdlatul-'Ulama, the United Moslem Party, the Christian Party, the Catholic Party, the Islamic Party and the Movement for the Defense of Indonesian Independence. The cabinet assumed office Mar. 20.

Data on Indonesia's major parties:

Nationalist Party—Formed in 1946 as a leftwing grouping by the merger of several nationalist groups. Advocated a neutralist foreign policy and a strong democratic form of socialism at home. Masjumi—Established in 1945 as a federation of Moslem organizations. Regarded as rightwing, advocated establishment of an Islamic republic; assumed a pro-West and anti-Communist stance in international affairs. Nahdlatul-'Ulama—Founded in 1926 as a non-political Moslem grouping, joined the Masjumi in 1946 but withdrew in 1952. Its religious outlook was ultra-orthodox; politically, it followed a strong pro-nationalist and anti-Western line. Christian Party—Founded in 1945, represented Indonesian Protestants, largely in the Moluccas, northern and central Celebes and northern Sumatra. Indonesian Socialist Party—Established in 1948 following a split in the Socialist Party, whose leftwing elements joined the Communist Party.

DISSOLUTION OF NETHERLANDS – INDONESIAN UNION

1951-56

The government of Pres. Sukarno, determined to rid Indonesia of all traces of the Netherlands' colonial presence, launched a concerted effort in 1951 to abolish the Netherlands-Indonesian Union, established by the 1949 Statute of Union. At an informal meeting with Dutch officials Aug. 16, the Indonesian delegate, Prof. Supomo, voiced Jakarta's view that the union must be dissolved because it represented "a vestige of colonial rule." Supomo proposed that the Statute of Union be replaced by "a normal international treaty." Supomo called the statute a "weapon to Communists and other extremists." No Jakarta government that advocated the Netherlands-Indonesian Union could have the support of the people, he declared.

Indonesia held a series of meetings with the Dutch to solve the dispute. But the talks proved inconclusive, and Indonesia unilaterally abrogated the union in 1956.

The first of the conferences to revise the Netherlands-Indonesian Union was held in The Hague Jan. 15-Feb. 29, 1952. (The meeting also dealt with the dispute over Dutch New Guinea.) Dutch and Indonesian representatives made considerable progress toward drafting agreements to replace the Statute of Union Charter, which governed trade, economic, military and cultural relations between the 2 countries. The talks, however, were temporarily suspended Feb. 29 after the Indonesian delegation was recalled to Jakarta following the resignation Feb. 25 of the cabinet of Premier Sukiman.

A joint communiqué issued in The Hague Mar. 2 cited the progress the 2 sides had made in the conference. It expressed hope that the tentative agreements reached on trade, balance of payments, investments and related matters would lead to a definitive solution.

Dutch-Indonesian discussions on replacing the Statute of Union were resumed June 29, 1954 at The Hague. An agreement to abrogate the Netherlands-Indonesian Union was reached and signed Aug. 9. The new pact would have placed the diplomatic, financial and economic relations between the 2 countries on a new basis. But the agreement proved abortive since it failed to receive the required ratification of the Indonesian House of Representatives.

The Dutch delegate at The Hague discussions, Joseph M. A. H. Luns, had conceded at a news conference Aug. 11 that the Netherlands-Indonesian Union "had never come to life" and, therefore, was nothing more than "an unsuccessful experiment." The Netherlands had agreed "without enthusiasm" to end the 2-nation partnership, Luns said. But since Indonesia regarded the union as a restrictive influence on its independence, Luns stated, the Netherlands had no choice but to agree.

Indonesia and the Netherlands resumed the discussions at The Hague Dec. 10, 1955. The talks were shifted to Geneva Dec. 16. A joint communiqué issued Jan. 4, 1956 said the 2 sides remained deadlocked over 3 principal issues: (1) the method of arbitrating differences in interpreting any future agreement reached by the negotiators; (2) whether Indonesian law would take precedence over an agreed treaty in the event of future political disagreement between the Netherlands and Indonesia; (3) whether Indonesia would recognize the rights and concessions granted to Dutch citizens by the former Netherlands East Indies government. The talks were adjourned Jan. 7 to permit both sides to consult their governments.

The conference resumed Feb. 7. The conferees reached agreement in principle on the dissolution of the union and on financial and economic matters. The talks, however, foundered on the question of a provisional pact for settling disputes, pending the drafting of a definitive solution. Indonesia proposed the establishment of an *ad hoc* committee of Dutch and Indonesian representatives to consider all disputes. Describing the proposal as too vague, Dutch delegates suggested an arbitration commission. Indonesia spurned the proposal, calling it stronger than the Union Court of Arbitration set up under the Statute of Union. Negotiations were broken off Feb. 11. The resumed talks had been sharply assailed both in the Netherlands and Indonesia. Dutch parliament members charged in foreign policy debate Dec. 23, 1955 that the resumption of the conference was premature and that there was no guarantee that agreements reached by the current Indonesian government would be honored by its successor.

The Moslem Association party in Indonesia, a member of the coalition government, had announced Dec. 6 that it would refuse to participate in The Hague negotiations. The Socialist and Nationalist parties charged that Dutch refusal to discuss Dutch New Guinea at the talks doomed The Hague conference to failure. 4 ministers resigned from the Indonesian cabinet Jan. 17, 1956 in protest against the Dutch-Indonesian discussions. The ministers were members of the Moslem Association and the Moslem Political Federation.

Indonesia Abrogates Union

In the wake of Dutch-Indonesian failure to reach agreement at The Hague talks, the Indonesian government Feb. 13, 1956 unilaterally abrogated the Netherlands-Indonesian Union. Indonesia formally informed the Netherlands of its action Feb. 21. A Dutch official described Indonesia's move as "unprecedented in international relations in peace-time and a bad example to the whole world."

The government's decision to abrogate the union was formally approved by the Indonesian House of Representatives Feb. 28. A 2d measure approved by the House Apr. 21 contained a series of amendments providing that: all agreements reached at the 1949 round-table conference at The Hague were revoked; the Dutch-Indonesian "relationship ... is henceforward an ordinary relationship as between fully sovereign nations based on international law"; all special privileges enjoyed by Dutch citizens in Indonesia were abolished, except for concessions for the operation of businesses that did not conflict with "the interests" of the Indonesian government.

A Netherlands protest note delivered to Indonesia Mar. 3 asserted that Jakarta's unilateral abrogation of the union was "at variance with international law." Indonesia Mar. 20 rejected the Dutch protest. The Jakarta government's note said Indonesia had no choice but to sever the union relationship on its own since all negotiations to accomplish this action bilaterally had failed.

The Dutch government announced May 4 that it had decided to change the status of its High Commissioner in Jakarta to that of an embassy.

Indonesia Repudiates Dutch Debt

The Jakarta government Aug. 4 announced its repudiation of all of Indonesia's debts to the Netherlands. Indonesia had acknowledged and accepted the debts in the round-table agreements. Finance Min. Wibisono explained that the debts were "of a political nature" and had been "imposed on Indonesia as a kind of compensation to the Netherlands in return for its consenting to recognize the sovereignty of Indonesia."

The Jakarta statement said Indonesia had owed the Netherlands 3.661 billion Dutch guilders (about $1.098 billion). Of this total, 661 million guilders ($198 million) had been used for economic development in Indonesia, but the remaining 3 billion guilders ($900 million) had financed "the war against ... Indonesia," the Jakarta statement said. Indonesia said it would continue to honor its debts to the U.S., Canada and Australia.

A Netherlands Foreign Ministry statement Aug. 7 recalled that at the 1949 round-table conference Indonesia had accepted the Dutch cancellation of 2 million guilders ($600 million) of Indonesia's total debt to Holland but had agreed to repay the remainder. A Netherlands protest note to Indonesia Aug. 10 charged that Jakarta's action was "a flagrant violation of the agreement which Indonesia has voluntarily concluded concerning the taking-over of part of the state debt."

STRUGGLE FOR DUTCH NEW GUINEA
1950-63

The 1949 Hague conference had granted Indonesia control of all Netherlands East Indies territories except Dutch (or West) New Guinea. The latter territory, lying just east of the Indonesian archipelago, consisted of the 160,618 square miles of the western half of the island of New Guinea plus several adjacent islands. The Netherlands, favoring ultimate self-determination for Dutch New Guinea's Papuans, resisted Indonesian claims to the territory—referred to by Jakarta as West Irian (Irian Barat). The 1949 conference, therefore, postponed further discussion of Dutch New Guinea's disposition until the following year. But both sides remained intractable when negotiations were resumed in 1950. Subsequent inconclusive talks were followed by a Dutch-Indonesian military confrontation in 1962. Renewed negotiations that year, under the aegis of the UN and the U.S., ended the fighting and put Dutch New Guinea under Indonesian control in 1963.

As administrator of the eastern half of New Guinea, Australia supported the Netherlands in the dispute. After Japan's defeat in World War II, eastern New Guinea had become a UN Trust Territory under Australian control in 1946. The area was later combined administratively with Papua, the southern half which had been occupied by Australian forces in 1914 during World War I, to form the Territory of Papua & New Guinea.

Dutch-Indonesian Conferences Fail

Dutch and Indonesian representatives held 2 separate conferences in 1950 in unsuccessful attempts to settle the dispute over the disposition of Netherlands-controlled Dutch New Guinea. The first series of meetings, of a joint Netherlands-Indonesian Commission, took place in the summer of 1950. The 2d conference was conducted at The Hague Dec. 4-27.

Following the conclusion of the summer discussions, the Netherlands' representatives Aug. 9 drew up a report opposing the transfer of Dutch New Guinea to Indonesia. The statement claimed that Dutch New Guinea's populace supported continued Netherlands rule and that Jakarta's possession of the territory would result in chaos and unrest that would cause "a rapid deterioration of all achievements in the past 50 years."

Indonesian Pres. Sukarno asserted in Jakarta Aug. 17 that his government still observed the 1949 Hague round-table agreement that called for a peaceful settlement of the Dutch New Guinea question. But he said Dutch control of the area constituted "an injustice that must be remedied." Sukarno warned that Indonesia would "fight till the end of time so long as one part of our country is not free."

At the Dec. 4-27 Hague conference, the head of the Indonesian delegation, Foreign Min. Mohammed Rum, insisted on the transfer of Dutch New Guinea sovereignty to Jakarta on the ground that it had been provided for under The Hague round-table agreements. Rum proposed that in exchange for Indonesian control of the territory, Jakarta would grant the Netherlands partial control of Dutch New Guinea's social, economic and cultural development and guarantee Dutch economic interests there.

The Netherlands delegate rejected Indonesia's claim; he argued that the 1949 Hague agreements had made no provisions for transfer of the territory to Jakarta. A compromise proposal by the Netherlands Dec. 26 suggested that Dutch New Guinea either be granted sovereignty under the Netherlands-Indonesian Union, while its administration remained Dutch, or that negotiations of the dispute continue under the auspices of the UN Commission for Indonesia or any other international body.

The Hague talks collapsed after the Indonesian delegation rejected the Dutch compromise proposal Dec. 27. The Indonesians emphasized that Jakarta would not enter into a "colonial relationship" with the Netherlands in regard to Dutch New Guinea. The Jakarta delegation reiterated that Indonesia would not recognize the continuation of "foreign domination" of a territory it regarded as part of Indonesia.

Indonesian claims to Dutch New Guinea had been opposed by Australian External Affairs Min. Sir Percy Spender and Herbert Evatt, deputy leader of the Labor Party opposition. Both men expressed their views in Australian House of Representatives debate Jan. 8, 1950. Spender argued that Indonesian control of Dutch New Guinea was not feasible since the territory's population was in the same state of development as those in neighboring Australia (East) New Guinea and adjacent islands. Evatt said it would be against the interest of the Papuans of Dutch New Guinea for an Asian race such as the Indonesians to be brought into their midst.

Indonesian and Netherlands officials conferred again in The Hague Jan. 15-Feb. 29, 1952, but these talks also failed. The Dutch refused to turn over Dutch New Guinea to Indonesia, and the Indonesians rejected a Netherlands' counterproposal to refer the matter to an international court for arbitration.

UN Opposes Dutch-Indonesian Talks

Faced with Netherlands refusal to engage in further discussions with Indonesia on the Dutch New Guinea dispute, Jakarta launched a campaign to bring the UN into the dispute. Indonesia finally succeeded in having the controversy placed on the agenda of the 12th UN General Assembly meeting Nov. 20-29, 1957. The Assembly, however, rejected an Indonesian resolution calling for further Dutch-Indonesian talks. The vote, cast Nov. 29, was 41-29 in favor of the resolution (11 abstentions), or 14 affirmative votes short of the ⅔ majority required for adoption.

The resolution was backed by most Arab-Asian and Soviet-bloc states; it was opposed by the Netherlands, Britain and France. The U.S. was among the 11 abstainers.

During Assembly debate, Netherlands delegate Carl W. Schurmann insisted that his government would not accede to Jakarta's demands for annexation of Dutch New Guinea "nor enter into any negotiations concerning the future status of that territory without its inhabitants having the right to decide on their own political future."

Indonesian Foreign Min. Subandrio asserted during the debate that Dutch New Guinea was an integral part of the former Netherlands East Indies, which had been recognized as Indonesia since 1948. The Netherlands, he said, had pledged to promote complete sovereignty for all the territories of Indonesia. Subandrio said The Hague's demand for self-determination for the people of Dutch New Guinea served only to confuse the issue since, he asserted, the principle of self-determination did not apply in this case.

UN Assembly action had followed the publication Nov. 6, 1957 of a Netherlands-Australian proclamation of common policy on New Guinea. The agreement provided for intensified social advancement of the New Guinea population and self-determination for the island. The joint statement said the Dutch and Australian governments would continue to "strengthen the cooperation at present existing between their respective administrations in the territories."

Ali Sastroamidjojo, Indonesia's chief delegate to the UN, charged Nov. 6 that the Netherlands-Australian statement was "an attempt to influence the peaceful solution of Indonesia's claim" to the territory.

Indonesia Takes Economic Reprisals

Following the UN General Assembly's refusal to discuss the Dutch New Guinea dispute, Indonesia launched a series of reprisals against Dutch economic interests in Indonesia, starting Dec. 1, 1957.

The government ordered a 24-hour strike Dec. 2 against Dutch-owned businesses in Indonesia. It simultaneously banned Dutch publications and the landing of Dutch KLM airliners at Jakarta. Indonesian union members Dec. 3 seized control of the Dutch KPM (Royal Interocean Lines) shipping firm, and import-export and machinery firms. The unions acted despite anti-seizure orders by the commander of the Jakarta army garrison. Worker seizures were extended Dec. 4 to 3 Dutch banks, including the Netherlands Trading Society, which controlled 70% of Indonesia's foreign trade.

The Indonesian government ordered the Netherlands Dec. 4 to close its consulates in Indonesia, and it simultaneously announced plans for the deportation of most of the 50,000 Dutch citizens living in Indonesia. Seizures of Dutch property throughout Indonesia continued Dec. 6-7.

Premier Djuanda disclosed Dec. 9 the government's seizure of all Dutch plantations in Indonesia, including their transport and equipment. Djuanda acted after Foreign Min. Subandrio had declared Dec. 3 that a peaceful solution of the Netherlands-Indonesian dispute was still possible, although Indonesia would not take the initiative toward a settlement. Subandrio objected Dec. 6 to a Dutch appeal to the North Atlantic Treaty Organization Council for Western "solidarity" in support of Holland in the New Guinea dispute.

The evacuation of Dutch citizens from Indonesia by plane and ships started Dec. 10, and 10,000 Dutch nationals left by Dec. 31. The Netherlands protested to members of the UN General Assembly and Security Council Dec. 23 against "injurious" treatment of Dutch nationals and the "wholesale spoliation" of their property by Indonesia. The Dutch statement termed the Indonesian actions an "illegal . . . challenge to the authority of" the UN as expressed in the General Assembly vote on West New Guinea.

The seized Dutch holdings, worth about $1½ billion, were nationalized by the Jakarta government under a bill passed by the Indonesian parliament Dec. 3, 1958. Additional Indonesian action against Dutch interests in 1958 included the withdrawal of oil concessions of BPM (subsidiary of Royal Dutch Shell) in the Sumatran provinces of Achin and North Sumatra (announced Feb. 3).

Further Indonesian moves against Netherlands interests were threatened by Pres. Sukarno Aug. 17, 1959. Sukarno warned that all Dutch capital and enterprises in Indonesia faced expropriation unless Indonesian claims to Dutch New Guinea were honored. Speaking at Jakarta ceremonies commemorating the "14th anniversary" of Indonesian independence, Sukarno said: (a) if "the Dutch remain stubborn," the history of Dutch enterprise would come "to a close on Indonesian soil"; (b) any foreign capital used with disregard for Indonesian needs would face seizure; (c) production of basic needs "shall be controlled by the state and . . . not . . . by private entrepreneurs"; (d) "whoever scoops up wealth at the expense of the public . . . will be punished severely and, if necessary, sentenced to death."

Netherlands Reinforces Dutch New Guinea

The Netherlands Apr. 27, 1960 announced plans to reinforce their forces in Dutch New Guinea with an aircraft carrier, an infantry battalion and jet fighters. The Netherlands parliament, by 71-47 vote May 10, upheld the military move despite an Indonesian note that warned May 3 against "playing with fire" by the "projected military challenge."

The Netherlands legation in Jakarta was invaded and sacked May 6 by 500 Indonesian students protesting the Netherlands military plans.

In reaction to the Dutch decision to reinforce the New Guinea garrison, Pres. Sukarno severed Indonesia's diplomatic relations with the Netherlands Aug. 17. Sukarno said he had acted because of The Hague's "persistent refusal" to turn over Dutch New Guinea to Indonesia. Sukarno recalled that Jakarta had sought to get the Netherlands to reverse its stand, first through a policy of "sweet persuasion" and then by pressure against Dutch economic interests in Indonesia. But the dispatch of additional Dutch forces to New Guinea, Sukarno asserted, made it impossible "to maintain any longer diplomatic relations with the Dutch."

Dutch Promote New Guinean Self-Rule

100,000 New Guineans voted Feb. 18-25, 1961 to elect 16 members of a 32-member Colonial Council. The Dutch governor was to fill the remaining 16 seats by appointment. The election, the first in the island's history, was the initial step of a Dutch plan to give the territory self-rule. Final results released Mar. 2 showed 12 Papuans and 3 Netherlanders elected. New balloting was scheduled for the 16th elective council seat since one of the Papuan candidates had been elected by 2 districts.

The Dutch government submitted to parliament in The Hague Mar. 1 a 10-year economic development plan to help Dutch New Guinea's 700,000 Papuans achieve independence. It called for annual expenditures starting at 100 million Dutch guilders (about $30 million) in 1961 and increasing each year to a level of 120 million guilders ($36 million) by 1964.

But Netherlands Premier Jan Eduard de Quay told the Dutch parliament Jan. 2, 1962 that his government had dropped its demands that Indonesia accept the principle of self-determination for Papuans in Dutch New Guinea as a condition for talks over the disputed territory. Indonesian Foreign Min. Subandrio Jan. 3 in effect rejected the implied Dutch offer of unconditional talks by insisting that the Netherlands turn over the territory to Indonesia prior to negotiations.

Subandrio disclosed Jan. 9 that Pres. Sukarno had set a deadline of "7 to 10 days" on diplomatic efforts to settle the dispute. Subandrio made the disclosure following a meeting of the West Irian (Dutch New Guinea) Liberation Supreme Command, at which Sukarno presided. At the meeting, Brig. Gen. Suharto, army Reserve Corps commander, was appointed as "theater commander" to head any possible military drive against Dutch forces. Suharto's headquarters was to be based in Macassar in South Celebes.

Dutch-Indonesian Naval Clash

The first Netherlands-Indonesian military confrontation over the New Guinea dispute occurred Jan. 15, 1962. The Netherlands navy reported from Hollandia, Dutch New Guinea Jan. 16 that Dutch destroyers had sunk 2 of 3 Indonesian torpedo boats intercepted Jan. 15 in Dutch New Guinea territorial waters in Etna Bay off the southeastern coast of Dutch New Guinea. The 3d boat was driven off. 53 Indonesian survivors were picked up by the Dutch. The Dutch announcement said that the Indonesian boats were heading toward the New Guinea coast and had provoked the attack by firing on a Dutch plane. The Dutch retaliated after the Indonesians ignored a warning shot, the Netherlands statement said. A further Netherlands report on the incident, issued Jan. 18, said that an Indonesian force of more than 100 men had been ordered to land near Kaimana, Dutch New Guinea and to "try to liquidate the Netherlands administration."

The Netherlands Mar. 11 released 52 of the 53 Indonesians captured in the Jan. 15 naval clash. The announcement was made by Acting UN Secy. Gen. U Thant, who had appealed to Dutch Premier de Quay Feb. 1 to free the Indonesians "as a humanitarian gesture." The 53d captive was in a Dutch hospital in Hollandia with injuries suffered in the clash.

Authorities in Dutch-controlled Biak island had reported Jan. 14 that about 200 Indonesian guerrillas had infiltrated Dutch New Guinea. The island's Dutch district officer said Dutch patrols had killed some of them. An Indonesian army spokesman had admitted Jan. 12 that Indonesian guerrillas were infiltrating the area. But he insisted that regular Indonesian forces were not involved.

Preliminary Peace Talks

Preliminary secret negotiations to settle the New Guinea dispute opened at an undisclosed site outside Washington Mar. 20, 1962. The talks followed Dutch and Indonesian acceptance of an appeal Jan. 17 by Acting UN Secy. Gen. U Thant that both sides settle their dispute peacefully at the conference table.

The meeting outside Washington was arranged by the U.S. It was attended by Dutch and Indonesian officials and ex-U.S. Amb. Ellsworth Bunker, who had been invited by U Thant to attend as a "3d party." The U.S. State Department had disclosed Mar. 13 that it had suggested the conference to the Dutch and Indonesian governments. Indonesian acceptance of the plan had been hastened by talks held by U.S. Atty. Gen. Robert F. Kennedy and Pres. Sukarno when Kennedy had visited Indonesia in February.

(A Dutch government communiqué issued Mar. 19 voiced concern at "a new and open threat to aggression"made by Sukarno "on the eve of the preliminary talks." Sukarno had declared in a Mar. 18 radio address that his Dec. 19, 1961 order for the "liberation" of Dutch New Guinea should be "intensified.")

The talks were recessed Mar. 23 and suspended Mar. 26 when Sukarno ordered the withdrawal of the Indonesian delegation.

Indonesia's reasons for withdrawing from the negotiations were explained by Foreign Min. Subandrio Apr. 2. He said: The Jakarta government had entered the talks "with the fair hope that the Netherlands would not reject in principle the transfer of administration [of Dutch New Guinea] under certain conditions which would reflect" Dutch "commitments" to Indonesia before 1950; "instead, even before the negotiations started, the Netherlands moved its warships from the Caribbean Sea to the Pacific Ocean, obviously on the first lap of their journey to West Irian"; Dutch "preparations in West Irian for the proclamation of a so-called independent Papuan State have been intensified"; the negotiations had "lost their secrecy and informality when the Netherlands" made announcements "more than once . . . as if real negotiations already had been started and as if" the negotiators "need not necessarily talk about the transfer of administration to Indonesia"; "the Indonesian delegate [Adam Malik] was told on more than one occasion [during the talks] that the Netherlands was not prepared to transfer administration over West Irian to Indonesia under any conditions"; "these combined factors compelled Indonesia to arrive at the conclusion that the meeting had been used by the Dutch merely as a tactical maneuver . . . to placate public opinion at home and to win support from the outside world . . . in their struggle against Indonesia"; Jakarta's creation of a "People's [military] Command" "was a reaction to Dutch preparations in West Irian to establish a so-called Papuan State."

Subandrio had disclosed Mar. 30 that Sukarno had received that day a letter in which U.S. Pres. John F. Kennedy expressed "a deep desire" "for resumption of secret talks [between the Netherlands and Indonesia] for a peaceful settlement" of the Dutch New Guinea dispute.

Dutch-Indonesian Fighting Renewed

With the collapse of the U.S.-sponsored Dutch-Indonesian negotiations, Indonesian armed forces renewed their drive for control of Dutch New Guinea. The military activity was resumed in late Mar. 1962. It reached its peak in May, then gradually diminished and was ended by a truce provided for under a definitive political settlement reached Aug. 15.

Among the military developments:

■ Dutch officials reported from Hollandia Mar. 28 that Dutch marines and policemen had fired on a band of 30 Indonesian soldiers invading Waigeo island, at the western tip of New

Guinea. The invaders fled, but some were captured later in a mopping-up operation.

■ A Netherlands military communiqué Mar. 30 said Dutch marines had fought and routed a group of Indonesian invaders Mar. 29 on Gag island, near Waigeo. The communiqué said that one Indonesian had been killed and that arms and ammunition had been captured.

■ Lt. Gen. Abdul Haris Nasution, Indonesian army chief of staff, announced in Bandung Apr. 2 that Indonesian guerrillas had landed at Sorong, Fakfak and Kaimana on the west and southwest coasts of New Guinea.

■ Maj. Gen. Ahmad Jani, chief of Indonesia's "liberation operations staff," announced Apr. 7 that Papuan "patriots" had seized control of the islands of Waigeo and Gag following skirmishes in which about 10 Dutch troops were killed or wounded. Jani said no Indonesian soldiers had been involved in the operation. The Dutch armed forces reported Apr. 9 the capture of 45 Indonesian infiltrators on Waigeo.

■ Rear Adm. Leendert Reeser, Dutch military commander in Dutch New Guinea, reported May 4 that Dutch marines had killed and captured several of a group of 25 Indonesian paratroopers who had been dropped Apr. 27 near Fakfak.

■ The Netherlands Defense Ministry reported May 15 that Indonesian paratroopers had been dropped that day from 4 planes in the Fakfak area. Other groups of Indonesian paratroopers were said to have landed May 15 and 17 near Kaimana. Netherlands officials announced May 17 that the Indonesians in the Fakfak area, including a group of 40 that had landed east of the town, had retreated before advancing Dutch marines. The Indonesian press agency Antara, reporting May 20 on the May 15 Fakfak action, said Indonesian units had killed 18 Dutch marines. This alleged Indonesian success was denied May 20 by the Netherlands Defense Ministry in The Hague.

■ The Dutch reported May 16 that their forces had captured a boat carrying 20 Indonesian soldiers as they were about to make a landing near Fakfak.

■ The Dutch reported May 19 that their forces had trapped about 200 Indonesian paratroopers in the Fakfak area.

■ Netherlands authorities reported May 20 that their units had killed 3 Indonesian paratroopers and wounded 3 others of a new group that had landed May 19 on the Vogelkop Peninsula, on the extreme western end of New Guinea. Indonesia confirmed May 21 that paratroop reinforcements had been dropped May 20 on the Vogelkop Peninsula as well as near Fakfak, Sorong and Teminabuan (Terminaboen). A broadcast heard in Tokyo May 21 quoted Antara as saying that Indonesian forces had captured Teminabuan "after a fierce battle."

■ Netherlands Premier de Quay told the Dutch parliament May 24 that Dutch forces had killed 22 Indonesian paratroopers in New Guinea and had captured 119.

■ A mopping-up operation against 5 scattered groups of Indonesian invaders was launched by Dutch soldiers, planes and ships May 25. Rear Adm. Reeser said a new pocket of 14 Indonesian paratroopers had been discovered. This brought the total number of known invaders to 580. The Dutch reported May 28 that their forces, supported by Papuans, had "isolated" all Indonesian paratroopers in Western Guinea.

■ Dutch military headquarters in Hollandia announced June 24 that an estimated 150-200 Indonesian paratroopers had been dropped near Merauke in the southeastern part of Dutch New Guinea. Merauke was the community in which the first Papuan political party in Dutch New Guinea had been established May 19; the party's platform opposed Indonesian claims to New Guinea.

■ Dutch Amb.-to-U.S. Jan H. van Roijen protested to Acting UN Secy. Gen. U Thant Aug. 10 over the landing of a group of 140 Indonesian invaders near Sorong Aug. 9. Dutch forces engaged the invaders Aug. 10.

■ 400-500 Indonesian paratroopers landed Aug. 14 near Merauke, Kaimana, Teminabuan and Sorong. Hollandia was placed on an alert, and the city's power supply was cut off.

Dutch Request UN Intervention

Indonesian Rep.-to-UN Sukardjo Wirjopranoto declared in New York May 18, 1962 that the Indonesian paratroop landings in Dutch New Guinea were the start of a "liberation" movement that would continue until there was a "peaceful solution" of the New Guinea dispute on Indonesia's terms. He made the statement after conferring with U Thant on a note Thant had received earlier in the day from Dutch Premier Jan Eduard de Quay. The note, made public May 21, called on Thant to urge Indonesia to stop "all aggressive action against Netherlands New Guinea." It declared that the Indonesian landings were "part of an act of aggression." De Quay requested that UN observers be sent to the area to prevent "further aggression."

In a note sent to de Quay May 23, Thant rejected the Dutch request. In a similar message dispatched to Pres. Sukarno, Thant declared that such intervention on his part would "imply that I was taking sides in the controversy." Thant urged both officials "to resume urgently the discussion which had been undertaken [in March] through the good offices of [U.S.] Amb. [Ellsworth] Bunker."

The presidents of 3 Papuan political parties sent telegrams to Thant protesting his rejection of the May 18 Dutch request that he send UN observers to New Guinea. The Papuans said: "The Indonesians are trying to subject our country and people by force while the United Nations neglects our rights as human beings. We are entitled to a just and strictly neutral investigation."

A Dutch note to Thant, made public May 25, said that documents taken from Indonesian prisoners in New Guinea "showed that the Indonesians involved in these landings from the air are members of the regular Indonesian military forces."

In a note delivered to Thant May 25 and made public May 28, Sukardjo Wirjopranoto justified Indonesian military moves in New Guinea on the ground that paratroopers who had been dropped there were not invaders but "Indonesian nationals who moved into Indonesia's own territory now dominated by the Dutch by force."

Thant, in notes sent to Dutch Premier de Quay and Pres. Sukarno May 29, appealed for a cease-fire in New Guinea pending negotiations between both sides. De Quay, in a reply received by Thant June 1 (made public June 2), said the Netherlands had "only made use of" its "right of legitimate self-defense in conformity" with the UN Charter.

Talks Resume, Dutch Agree to Cede Control

Ellsworth Bunker renewed his mediation efforts in the New Guinea dispute after further discussing the matter with U Thant May 23, 1962. Bunker later drew up a plan that provided for transferring the administration of Dutch New Guinea to Indonesia May 1, 1963 after temporary UN control of the territory. The Netherlands approved the plan May 26 "as a basis for negotiations" with Indonesia. Jakarta accepted "in principle" July 31.

Further discussions were held, and a formal agreement under which Holland was to relinquish Dutch New Guinea was signed by Netherlands and Indonesian representatives at UN headquarters in New York. Bunker acted as mediator of the negotiations on Thant's behalf. The talks were conducted on an estate near Middleburg, Va. The principal participants were Indonesian Foreign Min. Subandrio, Indonesian Amb.-to-USSR Adam Malik and Dutch Amb.-to-U.S. Jan H. van Roijen.

Under the agreement, Indonesia promised to arrange—by the end of 1969—a UN-supervised plebiscite in which the territory's 700,000 inhabitants, mainly Papuans, would decide "whether they wish to remain with Indonesia" or "to sever their ties with Indonesia."

The agreement provided for a cease-fire between Dutch and Indonesian forces, and the truce went into effect Aug. 17. (Brig. Indar Jit Rikhye of India, military adviser to UN Secy. Gen. U Thant, flew to New Guinea Aug. 21 to supervise the truce. He was to be assisted by 20-25 officers of the UN Emergency Force in the Middle East and the UN's Congo force. A UN force of about 1,000 men was to be sent to New Guinea to keep order during the transitional period. A UN spokesman Aug. 23 confirmed that Pakistan had agreed to Thant's request to supply the troops.)

Among other provisions of the agreement: (a) The Netherlands was to transfer West New Guinea Oct. 1 to a UN Temporary Executive Authority (UNTEA) that was to be "under the jurisdiction of the [UN] Secretary General"; (b) UNTEA's chief executive officer, a UN administrator, was to be appointed by Thant if found "acceptable" to Indonesia and the Netherlands; (c) Indonesia and the Netherlands would divide the cost of financing the 1,000-man UN force and other UN administration costs; (d) the UN force was to be used "primarily" to supplement the Papuan force; (e) Dutch forces were to be repatriated "as soon as possible," and Dutch forces in New Guinea awaiting departure were to be "under the authority" of UNTEA; (f) Indonesia's "primary task" after taking over West New Guinea "will be further intensification of the education of the people, of the combatting of illiteracy, and of the advancement of their social, cultural and economic development."

The Dutch-Indonesian agreement was accompanied by an exchange of letters in which the Netherlands and Indonesian governments resumed diplomatic relations, which had been severed Aug. 17, 1960.

Dutch Premier de Quay declared Aug. 15 that the Netherlands "had to sign" the New Guinea agreement because it "could not count on the support of its allies." De Quay's statement was in reference to reports that the U.S. had advised the Dutch that the U.S. 7th Fleet would not be used against Indonesia in the event that a full-scale war broke out over New Guinea. Dutch Foreign Min. M. A. H. Luns charged Aug. 16 that the U.S. had "drastically" "swung around" in its New Guinea policy and had acceded to Indonesian demands in the hope of keeping Indonesia out of the Communist camp.

The agreement was unanimously approved by the Indonesian parliment Sept. 1. The New Guinea Council approved the agreement the same day by 12-2 vote (6 Dutch and 3 Papuan members abstained), and the lower house of the Netherlands parliament approved the agreement by 127-9 vote Sept. 7.

The UN General Assembly approved the pact Sept. 21 by 89-0 vote (14 abstentions and 5 absent).

Dutch Rule Ends; Indonesia Takes Control

Netherlands rule over Dutch New Guinea, renamed West New Guinea, officially ended Oct. 1, 1962. The territory was formally transferred to UN control under a proclamation read in ceremonies in Hollandia by José Rolz-Bennett, who had been appointed by U Thant to head the territory's UN Temporary Executive Authority (UNTEA).

The UN in turn formally transferred West New Guinea to Indonesia May 1, 1963. These ceremonies were also held in Hollandia. Jakarta made the territory a province of Indonesia, renamed it West Irian and gave Hollandia the new name of Kotabaru.

In a message sent to be read at the latter ceremonies, UN Secy. Gen. U Thant expressed confidence that Indonesia would grant West Irian's Papuan population a plebiscite on self-determination before 1969, as stipulated in the Aug. 1962 transfer agreement.

Pres. Kennedy, in a message to Indonesian Pres. Sukarno, called the transfer of West Irian "a notable event both for Indonesia and the principle of peaceful settlement of disputes between nations." In a similar message to Sukarno, Soviet Premier Nikita S. Khrushchev hailed Indonesia's acquisition of West Irian as a victory in its "just struggle" for the territory. West Irian's newly-appointed Legislative Council assumed office May 2. Sukarno pledged in a message to the Council that he would use "all potentials of the Indonesian revolution" to raise the level of West Irian's backward areas. Sukarno said the take-over of West New Guinea was a step toward "wiping colonialism from the face of the earth."

Sukarno arrived in West Irian May 4 and said in a speech to a gathering of Papuans in Kotabaru: "We still must struggle to reach this goal" of justice and prosperity; "we must also struggle to reach our other goal of friendship with all nations"; having acquired West Irian, Indonesia had no desire to annex any other country or "to steal anything from anybody."

(Sukarno announced Apr. 19, 1965 that Indonesia would not allow a plebiscite in West Irian under which the Papuans could vote either to join Indonesia or become independent.)

SUMATRA & CELEBES REVOLTS

1956-61

The Indonesian government faced its most serious challenge since independence when rebellion against its authority flared in 1956 in Sumatra and Celebes. Government forces crushed the revolt after 5 years of bloody combat. The most intense battles were fought during 1958; rebel resistance began to crumble thereafter. After 3 years of minor sporadic clashes, the insurgents finally surrendered in 1961.

As in previous uprisings, the underlying cause of the unrest remained the unfulfilled demands of dissident military and political leaders for greater regional autonomy and a larger share of the national revenue. Further arousing the discontent of anti-government elements was a proposal enunciated by Pres. Sukarno in 1957 of a new political plan for Indonesia that he called "guided democracy." Its aim, according to Sukarno, was to curb the country's widespread political dissension and solidify the governmental structure.

Sukarno Decrees State of War

Sukarno decreed a state of war and siege in North Sumatra Dec. 25, 1956 and extended it to South Sumatra Dec. 28 following bloodless revolts by army and local officials against the central government.

Army forces led by Lt. Col. Achmad Hussein took control of Central Sumatra Dec. 20 and won a government pledge of "friendly relations" Dec. 31.

Rebel troops under Col. Maludin Simbalon, 37, took control of North Sumatra Dec. 22, established a Revolutionary Council and refused to negotiate with a government delegation Dec. 24. Pro-government army units under Lt. Col. Djamin Gintings were reported to have dispersed the North Sumatra rebels Dec. 27 and to have reoccupied Medan, provincial capital. Simbalon was reported captured by government forces Dec. 27, but he escaped Dec. 28.

Dispatches from Jakarta Dec. 29 reported another uprising on Celebes, where 163 rebels had been reported killed and 437 captured during fighting in June and July.

The Celebes army command and a 51-member council of army, police and civilian officials seized control of 4 eastern provinces on Celebes, the Moluccas and the Lesser Sundas (Bali and parts of Flores and Timor) in a revolutionary move Mar. 2, 1957 against the central regime.

The rebel action was led by Lt. Col. N. H. Ventje Sumual, Celebes army commander and head of the council. The South Sumatran army commander, Lt. Col. Barlian, also proclaimed Mar. 9 that he had taken control of the administration of that province. Indonesian Borneo's army commander, Lt. Col. Hasran Basri, announced Mar. 11 that a Revolutionary Council had been established to govern Borneo. The rebel actions were reported to be in opposition to the central government's handling of foreign exchange earned by exports from Indonesian areas beyond Java. The rebels also opposed the "guided democracy" plan, which Sukarno had announced Feb. 21.

The first bloodshed in the latest flare-up of revolt was reported Apr. 6, when rebels killed 29 soldiers and 2 civilians in an ambush 40 miles south of Macassar, South Celebes.

Premier Ali Sastroamidjojo and his coalition government, under attack for failing to halt the spreading revolt in Sumatra, resigned Mar. 14, 1957. Sukarno proclaimed a state of war and siege throughout Indonesia the same day. He declared that the government "is temporarily in my hands as head of state and supreme commander of the armed forces."

Sukarno Apr. 9 installed a 23-member "emergency extra-parliamentary cabinet of experts" headed by Djuanda as premier and interim defense minister.

Sumatra Rebels Proclaim National Regime

The Sumatra rebels defied the government's anti-insurgent measures and continued to consolidate their forces throughout 1957. Confident of their strengthened position, the rebels Feb. 10, 1958 issued an ultimatum demanding the dissolution of Djuanda's cabinet and the ouster of alleged Communist sympathizers from central government positions. The rebels called for the formation of a new central government headed by ex-Vice Pres. Mohammed Hatta and Sultan Hamengku Buwona of Jogjakarta. The rebels warned that if their demands were not met in 5 days the Sumatra Revolutionary Council would take action.

The central government rejected the rebel demands Feb. 11 and ordered the dishonorable discharge from Indonesia's army of these Sumatran insurgent leaders: Lt. Col. Achmad Hussein, Central Sumatra military commander; Col. Maludin Simbalon, ex-North Sumatra military chief; Lt. Col. Zulkifi Lubis, ex-acting chief of staff; Col. Dahlan Djambek, ex-deputy chief of staff and head of the Organization Against Communism in Central Sumatra.

A new revolutionary government for Indonesia was proclaimed Feb. 15 by rebel army and political leaders meeting in Central Sumatra. The new regime was headed by ex-Gov. Sjafruddin Prawiranegara of the Indonesian Central Bank as premier and finance minister. Prawiranegara was a Masjumi leader. The other cabinet members included Simbalon as foreign minister and Burhanuddin Harahap as foreign minister.

The proclamation announcing the formation of a revolutionary regime was issued after the expiration of the rebels' 5-day ultimatum. It said that the rebel cabinet would be prepared to transfer its authority to a government headed by Hatta and Hamengku Buwona if they expressed willingness "to establish a new government with sufficient guarantees" for accomplishing rebel aims.

Prawiranegara declared Feb. 15 that the rebel government was "not a separatist movement to disrupt the integrity of the Republic of Indonesia." He held that it represented "a struggle to establish a just and prosperous Indonesian state based on the belief in God Almighty." Prawiranegara said that although Sukarno had "forsaken his duty," the rebels would retain him as president if he took action to meet their demands.

The Indonesian army Feb. 16 ordered the arrest of Prawiranegara and 5 members of his cabinet on charges of intent to overthrow the Indonesian government by force.

Maj. Gen. Abdul Haris Nasution, army chief of staff, announced Feb. 17 the dishonorable discharges of Lt. Col. D. J. Somba and Maj. D. Runturambi, North and Central Celebes military commander and chief of staff, respectively, who had declared their support for the rebel regime the same day. Somba was ordered arrested for treason Feb. 18.

Sukarno returned to Indonesia Feb. 16 from a 5-week informal visit to Japan. He issued a statement in which he ignored the rebel government but professed belief that Indonesia would retain its unity under Jakarta.

The Jakarta government acted Feb. 17-18 to impose an economic blockade on the rebel regime by diverting all air and sea traffic to and from Sumatra and North Celebes. Gen. Nasution Feb. 18 ordered the abolition of pro-rebel councils in Central and South Sumatra and in Celebes.

Sukarno Feb. 21 rejected rebel demands for the ouster of Premier Djuanda. He called for measures to combat the rebel regime as a small group attempting to impose "their own egotistical desires on the nation." He cited "indications" that the rebels acted as "instruments of foreign powers" in their efforts to "make Indonesia ... join one bloc or the other." (Sukarno had met with Hatta in Jakarta Feb. 20 but apparently failed to win Hatta's approval for a proposed joint condemnation of the rebel regime. Hatta reportedly agreed that the rebels had "gone too far" in establishing a government, but he rejected condemnation of the rebel regime on the ground that it would "sharpen the situation.") Prawiranegara asserted Feb. 21 that Sukarno's statement would "close the door for further efforts at peaceful settlement. Violence is now possible." Prawiranegara denounced Sukarno as "unscrupulous" and said that the rebel regime would withdraw all loyalty to him as Indonesian chief of state.

Military Action Against Rebels

In the first military move against the rebel forces, Indonesian government planes bombed and strafed insurgent-held areas in Central Sumatra and North Celebes Feb. 21-22, 1958. Indonesian pilots, flying U.S.-built P-51 fighters and B-25 bombers, knocked out the rebels' main radio stations in

Padang and Bukittinggi, the rebel co-capitals, and reportedly destroyed another rebel transmitter Feb. 22 in Menado, North Celebes. The attacks, which followed an initial raid Feb. 21 against a bridge near Painan, Sumatra, also were directed against phone and telegraph centers in an effort to cut rebel communications.

The AP reported Feb. 25 that the rebel government had been moved to secret mountain headquarters in Central Sumatra to avoid new attacks.

The Indonesian navy began patrols off Padang Feb. 20 and blockaded the port against all Indonesian and foreign shipping.

The Indonesian army announced Feb. 27 that government troops had landed in North Celebes 125 miles from rebel headquarters in Menado. The Jakarta troops had been dispatched to reinforce pro-government militia and police units that had seized Gerontalo in rebel-controlled territory Feb. 25. Lt. Col. Ventje Sumual, rebel leader dishonorably discharged by the army Mar. 1, announced Mar. 3 that Gerontalo, center for 250,000 Gerontalese Moslems, had been retaken by rebels.

The Indonesian air force claimed Mar. 2 that a 3-day bombing campaign on ferries and rebel communications had "completely" cut off Padang.

Indonesian government soldiers launched an all-out invasion of Sumatra Mar. 7 in a major effort to put down the island rebellion. According to a rebel announcement Mar. 10, the first government landing on Sumatra Mar. 7 had been carried out by 300 paratroopers at Bengkalis, an island off the east coast of Central Sumatra. An Indonesian army report Mar. 11, confirming the landing, claimed the government troops had seized Bengkalis and 2 other nearby towns.

Government forces continued their build-up on Sumatra, and the fighting between rebel and government troops intensified. Government paratroops Mar. 12 captured Pakanbaru, 200 miles from the rebel capitals. But Col. Dahlan Djambek, rebel interior minister, claimed Mar. 11 that 150 of the 600 paratroopers dropped on Pakanbaru had been killed. Premier Djuanda asserted Mar. 13 that government troops had overrun U.S.-owned Caltex-Pacific Co. oilfields in the area. Another U.S.-owned oil firm, Standard Vacuum Oil Co. at nearby Lirik, was captured by government troops Mar. 23. Caltex-Pacific and Standard Vacuum resumed operations Mar. 24 after receiving assurances from Jakarta that shipping terminals at Pakning and Dumi would be protected from further military action.

Medan, North Sumatra was seized for the rebels by insurgent garrison troops Mar. 16. Padang radio said that 2,000 Sumatran soldiers had rebelled and had overcome Javanese troops commanded by Col. Djamin Gintings. Jakarta claimed Mar. 17 that loyal troops had regained control of Medan. Medan radio confirmed the government's claims Mar. 17, but rebel broadcasts said Mar. 18 that rebellious Moslem Achinese tribesmen had joined Sumatran forces to reopen the Medan battle. Jakarta said Mar. 19 that government troops controlled Medan and Pakanbaru despite rebel claims to have attacked both cities and retaken Medan Mar. 18. An Indonesian army spokesman said Mar. 21 that 300 rebels had been captured near Medan.

Government amphibious forces landed on the west coast of Central Sumatra Apr. 17 and captured Padang. Jakarta communiqués said that 6,000 troops had landed from an invasion fleet, one destroyer and 12 other ships and had seized Padang later the same day. Rebel troops and officials had evacuated Padang and had moved to Bukittinggi before the government forces landed.

Government forces began Apr. 18 to move on Bukittinggi, 60 miles inland from Padang; they advanced to within 15 miles of Bukittinggi by Apr. 22 despite strong resistance. Government planes bombed Bukittinggi Apr. 20-22 and Jakarta dispatches said Apr. 22 that the rebel government had fled to Batusangkar, 28 miles to the southeast.

(Lt. Col. Alex Kawilarang, Indonesian military attaché in Washington who had defected to the rebels, arrived in Central Sumatra Apr. 17 from North Celebes and reportedly assumed command of rebel military forces in Sumatra.)

Jakarta radio announced May 5 that Bukittinggi, the insurgent's 2d capital and the last major stronghold of the Central Sumatran rebel regime, had been occupied May 4 by the Indonesian army. Rebel leaders reportedly had fled to North Celebes, leaving only scattered rebel forces fighting in North and Central Sumatra.

Unsuccessful rebel efforts to negotiate a settlement were disclosed May 5 by Lt. Col. Rudy Pirngadie, an Indonesian army spokesman. He said that approaches by dissident Col. Joop F. Warouw had been rejected by Gen. Nasution, who insisted that the rebels must "surrender unconditionally" or be "crushed." Warouw was suspended May 5 as Indonesian military attaché in Peking for leaving his post and defecting to the rebels. Warouw was named commander of rebel forces in North Celebes May 6.

U.S. proposals for a negotiated cease-fire were confirmed by the U.S. State Department May 17. Jakarta dispatches reported May 16 that the U.S. peace plan had been presented to Indonesian Foreign Min. Subandrio May 14 by U.S. Amb.-to-Indonesia Howard P. Jones and had been rejected as "downright [U.S.] intervention" in the rebellion. Sukarno said at an East Java rally May 16 that "we will not negotiate with the rebels; we are gathering strength to crush the rebellion."

Fighting Shifts to Celebes

With the capture of the rebel co-capitals of Padang and Bukittinggi, the insurgents moved their seat of government to Celebes to continue their rebellion from there.

Rebel broadcasts from Menado, the capital, announced May 24, 1958 that a "caretaker cabinet" had been formed by Col. Joop F. Warouw, presumably to replace the scattered Central Sumatran government of Premier Sjafruddin Prawiranegara. Dr. Sumitro, a former member of the Sumatran rebel cabinet, was named foreign, finance and trade minister.

Indonesian government troops landed on the east coast of North Celebes June 16 and began a drive on Menado. The landings were made 20 miles east of the capital after smaller beachheads had been established by other army units on the west coast of the island June 9 and 13. Despite strong rebel resistance, government troops penetrated Menado's defenses June 19, and Jakarta announced the capture of the rebel capital June 26. Government communiqués claimed that the victory had "broken the back" of the revolt but warned that it did "not mean the rebellion has ended."

After losing Menado, the rebels withdrew their main

strength to Tondano, about 60 miles to the southeast. Government paratroops were dropped into 3 rebel-held centers in the Tondano area July 10, and they captured the city July 17. The operation was the last major battle fought between rebel and government soldiers.

Celebes Rebellion Ended

Although government forces captured the rebels' main stronghold in Celebes, the remnants of the insurgent army continued to hold out on the island, engaging government troops at infrequent intervals. The total collapse of the Celebes rebellion occurred Apr. 4, 1961 when 25,000 insurgents, led by ex-Col. Daniel Somba, surrendered in a formal ceremony at Amurang to Col. Sunander, the government's commander in North Celebes.

Pres. Sukarno Aug. 17 offered a general amnesty to members of rebel forces throughout Indonesia if they "surrendered unconditionally" and returned "to the fold of the republic" by Oct. 5. Mass rebel surrenders were reported in Sumatra by mid-September, and Sukarno began a program of political reorientation for ex-rebel leaders.

A government report said 25,000 Sumatran rebels and their leaders had surrendered. Among the leaders taken were Sjafrudddin Prawiranegara, president of the rebel regime, and his top aides, including Maludin Simbalon, Achmad Hussein and Zulkifi Lubis.

The casualties of the rebellion were never made public and the figures released by the government did not cover the entire period of the fighting. An Indonesian army official reported Apr. 2, 1959 that 106 rebels and 149 government troops had been killed in Central Sumatra between Mar. 16, 1958 and Feb. 28, 1959. A further report on 1959 casualties released by the government Dec. 16 said 13,354 persons had been killed in fighting that year on all fronts. Among those slain were 2,139 government troops, 7,500 rebels and 3,040 civilians. Gen. Abdul Haris Nasution, Indonesian defense minister, reported Aug. 17, 1961 that 4,107 government soldiers and 4,407 rebels had been killed during 1960 and the first 7 months of 1961.

International Developments & Arms Deals

The rebels and the Indonesian government sought U.S. and Communist arms during the height of the fighting in Sumatra and Celebes in 1958. A U.S.-Indonesian dispute arose over Jakarta's charges that American volunteers were fighting on the side of the rebels. Indonesia also accused Nationalist China of intervening on behalf of the insurgents.

Sumatran rebel Premier Sjafruddin Prawiranegara had warned Mar. 3, 1958 that the rebels would ask the U.S. for arms if the Sukarno government sought Soviet arms. Prawiranegara expressed doubt that Jakarta could retake rebel areas without Soviet arms aid. "It is not in the interest of the U.S. if this area becomes Communist," he warned.

U.S. State Secy. John Foster Dulles, speaking before the House Foreign Affairs Committee (testimony made public Mar. 9), said there was "a fair chance" that the Indonesian rebellion would bring "curtailment of the trend toward communism." Dulles said: "We would be very happy to see the non-Communist elements, who are really in the majority, . . . exert a greater influence" in Indonesia; Sukarno's "so-called guided-democracy theory" was a "nice-sounding name for what I fear would end up to be Communist despotism."

Dulles said Apr. 1 that the U.S. viewed the Indonesian rebellion as "an internal matter" and would remain neutral in its attitude toward the Jakarta and rebel regimes.

Indonesian Foreign Min. Subandrio asked the U.S. Apr. 8 to sell weapons to Indonesia. Subandrio assured U.S. Amb.-to-Indonesia Howard P. Jones that the arms would not be used against Sumatran rebels. He asked permission to buy $120 million worth of U.S. arms, planes and ships.

State Secy. Dulles asserted Apr. 8 that the U.S. would not supply arms "to either side" in the rebellion. Dulles disclosed that the U.S. had rejected Indonesian requests, made in July 1957, for $700 million worth of arms.

Dulles May 20 reiterated that the U.S. would not provide Indonesia with arms. He issued a statement in which he asserted that the rebellion was "an Indonesian matter," which should be settled "without intrusion from without."

Dulles' restatement of American policy was quickly followed

by a State Department disclosure May 21 that licenses had been granted for the export to Indonesia of $146,600 worth of U.S. small arms and nearly $1 million worth of aircraft and radio parts. Netherlands Amb.-to-U.S. J. H. van Roijen protested the arms sale. A State Department reply May 27 explained that the arms had been limited to police equipment purchased from private U.S. firms and not the U.S. government.

The Indonesian government disclosed Apr. 6 that arrangements had been made for the purchase of Soviet-bloc arms from Poland, Czechoslovakia and Yugoslavia. The government said that the purchases, reported to include 100 Czech aircraft, were unconnected with the revolt and had been made without political conditions.

The U.S. State Department expressed "regret" Apr. 7 that Jakarta had turned to the Soviet bloc "to buy arms for possible use in killing Indonesians who openly oppose the . . . influence of communism in Indonesia." Indonesian Premier Djuanda summoned U.S. Amb. Jones Apr. 9 to ask for "explanation and clarification" of U.S. statements opposing Indonesian arms purchases from the Soviet bloc.

Djuanda disclosed May 6 that the first shipment of Soviet MiG jet trainers, "3 or 4 of them," had arrived in Indonesia.

An agreement for the sale of an undisclosed amount of Soviet military equipment to Indonesia was signed in Moscow Jan. 7, 1961 by Lt. Gen. Abdul Haris Nasution, Indonesian defense minister, and Soviet First Deputy Premier Anastas I. Mikoyan. Nasution told newsmen on his return to Jakarta Jan. 16 that the arms pact had "doubled our military strength." Indonesian sources reported that the agreement covered the purchase of $400 million worth of aircraft, submarines and torpedo boats.

Premier Djuanda charged Apr. 30, 1961 that U.S. and Chinese Nationalist "adventurers" had been hired by the rebels as pilots to fly combat missions against government forces. Djuanda said he had "proof" that arms and planes had been smuggled to the rebels from Taiwan as part of "overt foreign assistance" to anti-Jakarta forces. U.S. Pres. Eisenhower conceded Apr. 30 that "soldiers of fortune" usually were attracted to any rebellion. But he insisted that U.S. "policy is one of careful neutrality" toward the Indonesian conflict. The Chinese Nationalist government denied May 3 that it had aided the rebels, either with men or equipment.

Indonesian Foreign Min. Subandrio said May 8 that he had reached agreement with U.S. Amb. Howard P. Jones on the prevention of foreign intervention in the Indonesian civil war. Jakarta officials said May 9 that the talks had centered on Indonesia's request for U.S. pressure to halt Chinese Nationalist provision of arms, fuel and pilots to the rebels.

Further Indonesian charges of Nationalist Chinese intervention in the rebellion were made May 17 by Ganis Harsono, a spokesman in the Foreign Ministry. Harsono claimed that a Chinese Nationalist battalion had been seen aiding rebel forces in North Borneo.

Jakarta government officials said May 19 that Communist China had offered to send thousands of "volunteers" to help Indonesia suppress the rebellion. They said the Sukarno government had not accepted the unsolicited Chinese offer. The Chinese offer had been broadcast May 15 by Peiping radio. An official statement said China was prepared to send "further assistance" as "requested by the Indonesian government." It indicated that such aid could include military equipment for use against the rebels. Foreign Min. Subandrio met May 16 with the Chinese Communist and Soviet chargés d'affaires to discuss alleged foreign intervention in the Indonesian rebellion.

Indonesians Capture U.S. Pilot

An ex-U.S. Air Force officer flying for the rebels—Allan Lawrence Pope, 30, of Miami, Fla.—was shot down and captured by Indonesian government forces May 18, 1958 while piloting a U.S.-built B-26 bomber in an attack on Ambon harbor in the Moluccas. According to a Jakarta announcement May 27, Pope, who had been a pilot for the Chinese Nationalist Civil Air Transport on Formosa, had been flying for the rebels since Apr. 21 for a $10,000 monthly salary.

Pope went on trial before a Jakarta military court Dec. 28, 1959 on charges of causing the deaths of 17 Indonesians in raids flown for the rebels. He was convicted and sentenced to death Apr. 28, 1960. Pope denied making any bombing raids before the May 18, 1958 attack in which he was downed. He also denied that he had been paid for flying for the rebels. Pope insisted that his only motive for serving with the insurgents was to fight Communists. The court rejected Pope's request that he be considered a prisoner of war on the ground that Indonesia was not in a state of war with any country.

Pope's death sentence was later commuted to life in prison. Pope was released from jail July 2, 1962 under a general amnesty and was returned to the U.S.

'GUIDED DEMOCRACY' & SUKARNO'S POWER
1957-63

Taking note of the unabated unrest in Indonesia since it had become an independent country in 1945, Pres. Sukarno Feb. 21, 1957 proposed a "guided democracy" plan to provide greater stability. Asserting in a broadcast that Western-style parliamentary democracy was not "a true democracy in accordance with the ideals of the Indonesian people," Sukarno declared the time ripe to establish a governmental system "new in every respect." Sukarno's rejection of Western-style democracy came at a time when he was forming ever-closer ties with leaders of other "neutralist" nations and, according to many observers, seemed to be making a bid to assume the leadership of a "3d force" independent of both sides in the "cold war." Such a force, it was thought, might hold the balance of power between East and West and thereby control important decisions in world affairs.

Sukarno's plan called for the formation of (a) a new cabinet made up of representatives of all parties with seats in parliament, and (b) a National Advisory Council. The council, of which Sukarno would be chairman, would represent all groups and elements in Indonesian society: workers, peasants, businessmen, the armed forces and religious organizations. The council would advise the cabinet. Parliament would retain its functions, but the cabinet, in effect, would represent parliament. Sukarno defended the inclusion of the Communist Party in the cabinet on the ground that one could not "ignore a party that won 6 million votes in the general elections." Refuting criticisms that he sought "to bring the cabinet to the left," Sukarno insisted that his plan was aimed only at bringing about greater stability.

Sukarno had criticized Indonesia's parliamentary system at a news conference Jan. 17. "Democracy in Indonesia, if left to its present course, will not achieve the results we hope for," Sukarno warned. "On the other hand, our centuries-old inheritance of democracy as practiced in the villages—known as *musjawarah*, which means 'discussion,' and *gotong royong*, which means 'collective and mutual help'—will be a big asset for the basis of our democracy . . . ." Sukarno said that his recent plea to political party leaders to "bury all parties" was a warning to them "that they cannot go on this way, ignoring the needs . . . , hopes and disappointments, of the teeming millions just because there is disagreement among the leaders at headquarters." He promised that "in no way" would his proposal result in "a dictatorship." But, he warned, "to allow unfettered opposition to get an absolute majority will only degenerate into a mere struggle for the elimination of political opponents."

Although he said he disapproved of a resort to arms in Sumatra to back demands for greater autonomy, Sukarno expressed the view that there was "no escape for Indonesia otherwise than by a system of local autonomy for the various regions."

Sukarno Assumes Wide Powers

In a move to advance his plans for "guided democracy," Sukarno called Feb. 20, 1959 for the restoration of the 1945 provisional constitution. The old charter had been replaced by a new one when Indonesia became a unitary state in 1950. Sukarno said that the 1945 charter, providing for strong presidential powers, would be complemented by bills to reduce the large number of Indonesian political parties and to permit the formation of "functional groups," including the army and labor, in parliament. Sukarno's proposals had been approved at meetings of Premier Djuanda's cabinet Feb. 19 and of army leaders Feb. 18.

Sukarno assumed near-dictatorial powers July 5 when he decreed the reinstatement of the 1945 constitution.

Sukarno acted in defiance of the Constituent Assembly, which had voted 3 times—May 30, June 1 and June 2—to reject his demands for special powers to carry out his program for guided democracy. Sukarno each time got 47 to 49 votes fewer than the required majority. His defeat in the Assembly was traced to the opposition of the 2 major Moslem parties, the Masjumi and Nahdlatul-'Ulama. Premier Djuanda had warned the Assembly June 1 that failure to grant Sukarno the powers requested could result in military rule. All Indonesian political activities were banned on orders of Lt. Gen. Abdul Haris Nasution, army chief of staff, following the final Assembly vote June 2. Acting as central war administrator in the absence of Sukarno (who was visiting the U.S. at the time), Nasution banned all public and private meetings, demonstrations or other actions that "might influence or decide the course of the Indonesian state."

The powers assumed by Sukarno July 5 were detailed in a 2-part decree read by him that day to a gathering in front of the Presidential Palace in Jakarta. The decree (1) dissolved the Constituent Assembly and (2) replaced the 1950 provisional constitution with the 1945 charter. Sukarno declared that he had acted only after a majority of Assembly members had boycotted sessions, and "it was no longer possible for the Constituent Assembly to conclude the task entrusted to it." Sukarno said that his action was the "only way possible to save the state" and had the "support of the majority of the Indonesian people."

Sukarno said that he would name a new Provisional People's Consultative Assembly made up of parliament members and representatives of regional and functional groups. The 1945 constitution concentrated all executive and cabinet powers in the president and made him accountable only to the Consultative Assembly, which was required to meet at least once every 5 years. The constitution gave Sukarno full legislative powers, subject to parliamentary approval.

An order issued July 5 by Lt. Gen. Abdul Haris Nasution directed Indonesia's armed forces to obey the Sukarno decrees. The decrees were said to have been issued only after Nasution and other military leaders had assured Sukarno of their support.

(Nationalist and Communist newspapers generally approved Sukarno's action July 6. Moslem newspapers expressed opposition.)

Sukarno July 6 accepted the resignation of Premier Djuanda

but ordered him to remain as caretaker premier until a new cabinet was formed.

Sukarno July 8 appointed a 10-member "inner cabinet" in which he assumed the additional post of premier. Ex-Premier Djuanda became first minister and Lt. Gen. Abdul Haris Nasution was named security and defense minister. Sukarno administered the oath of office to his cabinet July 10. He announced that it would remain in office for at least 5 years to implement his guided-democracy plans. Sukarno completed his cabinet July 12 with the appointment of an "outer cabinet" of 29 deputy ministers. Only 2 of the deputies, Education Min. Prijono and Mobilization Min. Sudjono, were regarded as pro-Communist.

Sukarno's assumption of revolutionary powers was approved by acclamation by parliament July 22. Only leaders of the Masjumi party protested. They said Sukarno's decrees were an "act of force" and illegal. Sukarno reinstalled 236 parliament members July 23 under an oath of loyalty to the 1945 constitution.

The National Advisory Council proposed by Sukarno Feb. 21, 1957 came into being July 30, 1959. A 77-member National Planning Council was also established. The 44-member Advisory Council included Sukarno as its head, Communist Party Secy. Gen. Dipa N. Aidit and leaders of 8 other parties. The opposition Masjumi party was excluded. Ex-Foreign Min. Ruslan Abdulgani was named advisory council vice chairman, and Social & Cultural Affairs Min. Mohammed Yamin was appointed planning council chairman.

Sukarno further strengthened his rule Jan. 13, 1960 by issuing decrees granting himself wider powers. The decrees gave him the power to: (1) ban or dissolve any political party that failed to support the Indonesian state or the Sukarno regime, that did not have active branches in at least 1/4 of Indonesia's provinces and did not exclude members of any rebel group; (2) establish and lead a National Front to "mobilize and to unite all 'revolutionary forces' in Indonesia and to work closely with the government in all matters" in order to "complete the national revolution"; (3) appoint and dismiss members of a 3-year Provisional People's Consultative Assembly, to function as

Indonesia's "supreme state body." (The new Provisional Assembly was to contain 270 members of the current parliament, 200 representatives of functional groups and 94 regional representatives.)

Sukarno Dissolves Parliament

Pres. Sukarno dissolved parliament Mar. 5, 1960 because of its opposition to his plans for guided democracy. He appointed a new "self-help" parliament Mar. 27.

In dissolving the previous parliament, Sukarno charged Mar. 5 that the 257-member body, elected in 1955 under the 1950 constitution, had not satisfied his "expectations of . . . mutual assistance between government and parliament" following his assumption of special powers and resurrection of the 1945 charter in 1959. He asserted that parliamentary opposition had endangered "unity and security of the state" and had hampered "achievement of a just and prosperous society."

Parliament's dismissal left only these Indonesian governmental bodies, all appointed by Sukarno: the 39-member cabinet; the 45-member Supreme Advisory Council; the 77-member National Planning Council.

Sukarno installed the new parliament in Jakarta June 25, 1960. In an address at the opening session, Sukarno made it clear that its powers would be consultative rather than legislative and that he would exercise final power over all parliamentary decisions. The legislative body consisted of 283 members. 50%, including 62 Communists and 80 Moslems, were named from political parties. The others were chosen from "functional groups," such as the army, labor and youth organizations. Sukarno had named 16 more Moslems to the new body June 17 in response to protests that it was weighted in favor of Communists and leftists.

Dr. Sartono, a Nationalist Party leader, speaker of the old parliament and former Sukarno associate, had refused an appointment to the new parliament June 7. The anti-Communist Democratic League, formed by the Moslem, Roman Catholic and other parties opposed to the new parliament, reportedly was warned by First Min. Djuanda June 24 to disband or face forcible dissolution.

Communist dissatisfaction with the new parliament had been voiced Apr. 1 by Communist Party Secy. Gen. Dipa N. Aidit, who demanded elections "right away" and claimed that Communists "could get at least 10 million votes if free elections — and not a swindle — were held now."

Sukarno Aug. 15 established a 61-member governing council of the National Front and a 609-member Provisional People's Congress. The power to create these bodies were incorporated in the decrees Sukarno had issued Jan. 13, 1960. The National Front council included ex-Premier Ali Sastroamidjojo of the Nationalist Party, Chrmn. Idham Chalid of the Orthodox Moslem Scholars Party and Secy. Gen. Chrmn. Dipa N. Aidit of the Communist Party but no members of any opposition group. The Congress, named from among 283 members of parliament and 326 new appointees, represented Indonesia's 22 provinces and 16 "functional groups." Under the restored 1945 constitution, the Congress was empowered to fix broad outlines of national policy and elect the president and vice president. Sukarno Nov. 8 appointed Development Min. Chaerul Saleh as acting Congress chairman.

Sukarno Suspends Political Parties

Sukarno Sept. 13, 1960 ordered the suspension of all political party activities. The suspension reportedly was intended (1) to preserve the current Indonesian political balance until a decree insuring Sukarno's control of all political groups became effective Dec. 1, and (2) to halt the suppression of Communist Party activities by Gen. Nasution, army chief of staff, and other anti-Communist military leaders.

Sukarno Aug. 17 had ordered the dissolution of the Socialist and Masjumi parties on the ground that they were "clearly counter-revolutionary." The 2 parties announced Sept. 16 that they were disbanding in compliance with the order.

Press regulations published Oct. 12 banned all but "constructive" criticism of Sukarno's policies and ordered all publications to publicize government aims and policies. Under decrees issued by Sukarno as supreme war administrator, 8 newspaper plants had been seized Sept. 25 and 27. The seizures closed *Pedoman* (the country's largest daily) and *Nusan-*

tara, the only remaining anti-Communist paper.

Sukarno Apr. 15, 1961 signed a decree limiting the number of political parties to 8. Sukarno explained that the purpose of the action was to "simplify" the nation's party system. Applications of 4 splinter groups and the anti-Communist Masjumi and Socialist parties for authority to be legal parties were rejected. The parties allowed to exist were Communists, Nationalists, Orthodox Moslem Scholars, Catholics, Islamic Association, Murba (pro-Communist), Partindo and League for Upholding Indonesian Independence. The decree gave the president power over all political organizations and said any party could be abolished if it failed to follow the government's "left progressive ideology."

8-Year Development Plan Enacted

The National Planning Council announced Aug. 13, 1960 an 8-year economic development plan for Indonesia. The 240 billion-rupiah ($5.4 billion) program went into effect Jan. 1, 1961. The plan called for an investment of an estimated 13% of Indonesia's 236 billion-rupiah annual national income in order to achieve an 11.6% increase in national income by 1969. An estimated $1 1/2 billion in foreign aid was needed to help finance the project.

Oil and natural gas exploitation, refining, transportation and sales were to be turned over to state companies or private firms working under government contracts under legislation signed by Sukarno and published Nov. 1. The law provided that foreign oil and gas firms would be permitted to continue operations in Indonesia as contractors. All foreign mining concessions were declared invalid, but concessionaires were given similar assurances.

Land reform regulations promulgated Jan. 1, 1961 by Sukarno and made public Jan. 3 were intended to transfer at least 2 hectares (4.9 acres) of land to each family of Indonesia's landless farm population of 42 million.

Sukarno Appointed President for Life

The Provisional People's Congress May 18, 1963 appointed Sukarno as president of Indonesia for life. In accepting the decision of the Congress, Sukarno said at a Bandung rally

May 20 that "it would be well if an elected People's Congress would review the matter in the future." Sukarno said he accepted the life presidency to continue "to give leadership to the revolutionary struggle of the people of Indonesia."

Sukarno Escapes Assassination Attempts

Pres. Sukarno escaped 4 assassination attempts in 1957, 1960 and 1962.

In the first incident, Nov. 30, 1957, hand grenades were thrown at Sukarno while he was visiting a school celebration in Jakarta. Sukarno escaped injury, but 5 children and 2 of his aides were killed. 150 persons, mostly children, were injured. Indonesian authorities subsequently arrested 20 persons for alleged involvement in the attack.

In the 2d episode, 2d Lt. Daniel Mauker, 28, flying an Indonesian MiG-17, strafed the Presidential Palace in Jakarta and Pres. Sukarno's residence in nearby Bogor Mar. 9, 1960 in an attempt to kill Sukarno. Sukarno was not hurt, but 18 persons were wounded in the attack on the 2 buildings. Mauker was captured after he parachuted from the jet over West Java. Mauker was sentenced to death by a Jakarta court-martial July 15, but the execution was not carried out.

Sukarno escaped injury Jan. 7, 1962 when a grenade exploded a few hundred yards behind a motorcade in which he was riding in Macassar in South Celebes. 3 persons were killed and 28 injured. Sukarno said Jan. 8 that an investigation had shown that the grenade attack had been "perpetrated by agents of the Dutch" in an attempt to assassinate him. Several persons were arrested in Macassar in connection with the incident.

Sukarno again escaped injury May 14, 1962 when a gunman tried to shoot him during a religious ceremony in a Jakarta square. A Jakarta broadcast reported that: 5 persons, including Parliament Speaker Sainul Arifin, were slightly injured; the assailant, who was "arrested immediately," was one of 9 men ordered by Karto Suwirjo, leader of the Darul Islam, to kill Sukarno.

'CRUSH MALAYSIA' CAMPAIGN

1963-66

Malayan Prime Min. Abdul Rahman had conceded May 27, 1961 that "Malaya today as a nation realizes she cannot stand alone and in isolation." He suggested that "sooner or later she [Malaya] should have an understanding with Britain" and its colonies of Singapore, North Borneo, Brunei and Sarawak on the establishment of some form of a cooperative political and economic structure. Tungku (Prince) Abdul Rahman's suggestion was the first public proposal that eventually led to the formation of the Malaysian Federation in 1963. But it soon became evident that the creation of the new federation would interfere with the plans of Indonesian Pres. Sukarno, who thereupon organized a campaign to "crush Malaysia."

Indonesia's objections to the proposed Malaysian Federation were summed up in a statement by Sukarno: "We Indonesian people not only disagree with Malaysia but we oppose it at all costs. Malaysia was created by the British to encircle Indonesia" and thus was "endangering the Indonesian revolution." Indonesia sought to frustrate Malaysia's creation and fought it militarily after it was established, but to no avail. Finally, rocked by internal disorders, Indonesia made peace with Malaysia in 1966.

The groundwork for the proposed federation was laid at a meeting of Rahman and Singapore Prime Min. Lee Kuan Yew Sept. 19-20, 1961. The 2 leaders agreed on plans for the merger of their territories. This meeting was followed by conferences of Rahman and British officials in 1962. At the last round of these discussions, held in London Nov. 20-22, 1962, Rahman and British Prime Min. Harold Macmillan formally agreed to the formation of the Malaysian Federation. Brunei, North Borneo and Sarawak, which bordered on Indonesian Borneo, were to be given their independence on joining the new nation. (Brunei subsequently decided not to join.)

3-Nation Manila Conference

The leaders of Indonesia, Malaya and the Philippines met in Manila July 30-Aug. 5, 1963 to discuss the dispute arising over the proposed federation of Malaysia.

The conference dealt largely with Indonesian and Philippine demands for a UN survey to determine whether recent elections held in Sarawak and North Borneo represented genuine majority support for their membership in the proposed federation. An agreement accepting this demand was signed at the conclusion of the conference Aug. 5 by Indonesian Pres. Sukarno, Philippines Pres. Diosdado Macapagal and Malayan Prime Min. Abdul Rahman. The agreement implied that Indonesia and the Philippines would resubmit their demands for a referendum in Sarawak and North Borneo if the UN observers found fault with the previous elections held there.

(The 3 Asian leaders also signed a "Manila Declaration" that established a permanent consultative body to take up matters of mutual political, economic and military interest in the area. The new organization was to be known as Maphilindo, a combination of the names of the 3 nations.)

UN Secy. Gen. U Thant agreed to the Manila conference's request for a UN-conducted survey in Sarawak and North Borneo, and the canvassing started Aug. 26. Reporting on the results Sept. 14, Thant said "a sizeable majority" of persons interviewed in the 2 territories favored joining the federation. The UN survey team had been accompanied by 4 Malayan and 4 British observers. Indonesia and the Philippines refused to be represented after Jakarta's demands for 10 observers for each nation had been rejected.

Federation Formed; Ties with Jakarta & Manila Cut

The Federation of Malaysia formally came into being Sept. 16, 1963. Ceremonies proclaiming its establishment were held simultaneously in the new union's 4 territories — Malaya, Singapore, Sarawak and North Borneo (renamed Sabah). The seat of power was to be in Kuala Lumpur, where the Malayan parliament was to be expanded to include representatives from the 3 other states. Although the 4 former British territories became independent, Britain retained its military bases in Singapore and Malacca and was treaty-bound to defend Malaysia, as were Australia and New Zealand. Malayan Premier Abdul Rahman automatically became premier of Malaysia and was inaugurated in Kuala Lumpur.

Malaysia severed diplomatic relations with Indonesia and the Philippines Sept. 17. Rahman said Malaysia had "no choice" because Indonesia had broken ties with Malaysia "without any apparent reason" and because Manila's request to reduce its embassy in Kuala Lumpur was "not acceptable." Anti-Indonesian demonstrators had atacked Jakarta's embassy in Kuala Lumpur earlier Sept. 17.

Indonesian and Philippine refusal to recognize the Malaysian Federation had been announced Sept. 15. Indonesia Foreign Min. Subandrio said his country would withhold recognition until the UN had made "corrections" in its August survey in Sabah and Sarawak to determine whether the 2 territories wanted to join the federation. Subandrio said the UN survey was "not in accordance" with the principles outlined by Malaya, Indonesia and the Philippines at the July 30-Aug. 5 Manila conference. The Philippine Foreign Office said the Malayan embassy in Manila would revert to consular status until the Philippines recognized the federation. The Philippine ambassadors in Kuala Lumpur and Jakarta were recalled.

Violent Reaction in Indonesia

The formation of the Malaysian Federation precipitated immediate violent reaction in Indonesia. Jakarta's anger was directed particularly toward the British for their support of Malaysia.

About 5,000 Indonesian demonstrators attacked the Malayan and British embassies in Jakarta Sept. 16, 1963. After stoning the Malayan embassy, the demonstrators stormed the British embassy and smashed windows, ripped down an iron fence, burned Amb. Andrew A. Gilchrist's car and tore down the British flag. Indonesia seized the British embassy Sept. 18 after more than 10,000 demonstrators had sacked and burned the building that day. The Jakarta homes of British embassy staff members also were raided. The British Cricket Club and the Shell Oil Co.'s residential compound in the suburb of Kebajoran were burned. 19 British-owned cars were set afire.

Martial law was declared in Jakarta, and Indonesian troops took up positions in the city to restore order. The Jakarta military garrison broadcast a public appeal to stop "illegal action, disorder, seizure of property, molesting of people [and] strikes. . . ."

The Indonesian government action followed a protest delivered by British Foreign Secy. Lord Home to Indonesian Amb. Durhanudin Mohammed Diah in London. Home demanded that "such uncivilized behavior should be stopped forthwith" and that British lives and property be protected. An Indonesian reply delivered by Diah to Home Sept. 19 said the Jakarta government deplored the violence and would guarantee the safety of British nationals and properties in Indonesia. A British note handed to Indonesian Chargé d'Affaires Suryo di-Puro in London Sept. 23 demanded "full compensation" for damage to the British embassy in Jakarta and British homes in Indonesia.

It was reported Sept. 19 that Indonesian unions had seized and turned over to the government British-owned rubber, tea, coffee and palm-oil plantations and other properties in Sumatra and Jakarta.

Pres. Sukarno Sept. 20 ordered the seizure of all British-owned properties in Indonesia (value: more than $500 million). Asserting that the move was not a preliminary to nationalizing the firms, Sukarno said his order would insure the companies' safety and uninterrupted production and prevent their seizure by leftwing unions. The British Foreign Office Sept. 20 expressed concern over Sukarno's actions. The Foreign Office complained that Indonesia had not "satisfactorily" explained when the "rightful [British] owners would regain possession of their properties."

It was announced in Kuala Lumpur Oct. 31 that Britain had suspended further aid to Indonesia under the Colombo Plan pending an improvement in relations between Britain and the Jakarta government. Other British aid projects to Indonesia already started were unaffected.

U.S. government officials announced Sept. 24 that the

Johnson Adminstration would temporarily withhold all new economic assistance to Indonesia in view of Jakarta's anti-British behavior and its severance of diplomatic relations with Malaysia. (Current U.S. aid to Indonesia totaling $70-$80 million annually was unaffected.)

U.S. State Secy. Dean Rusk told Indonesian Foreign Min. Subandrio in New York Sept. 24 that the U.S. was concerned over the seizure of the British embassy and had a "strong interest" in a peaceful solution of the Indonesia-Malaysia dispute. The U.S. State Department had reported Sept. 19 that U.S. Amb. Howard P. Jones Sept. 18 had "made strong representations to Pres. Sukarno over the outrageous incidents of the past few days, including the burning of the British embassy."

Sukarno charged Sept. 25 that Indonesia was threatened by "Malaysian neo-colonialism" and would have to "fight and destroy" the 4-nation federation. Sukarno challenged the UN survey on Sarawak and Sabah. He charged that the questioning had been conducted "under guard of bayonets." Sukarno complained that the UN survey team had not employed the procedures agreed to by Indonesia, Malaya and the Philippines at their August meeting in Manila.

A decree issued by Sukarno Nov. 6 ordered the seizure of all Malaysian-owned rubber milling plants in East Sumatra. The order followed reports that Chinese merchants were planning to smuggle milled rubber in the area to Singapore and Penang, Malaya.

First Military Clashes

The first military clash caused by Indonesia's dispute with Malaysia took place Sept. 24, 1963. A British army spokesman reported that a Sarawak village had been hit by 4 mortar bombs that day fired from the Indonesian Borneo border. An Indonesian force of 40 men was said to have fired on an 18-man army patrol near the Sarawak town of Lubok Antu Sept. 28. An army spokesman said the attackers fled after a 15-minute exchange of fire. The Indonesian marine corps disclosed Sept. 29 that it had sent a commando unit to reinforce regular troops along the border.

UN Secy. Gen. U Thant Dec. 31 received a Malaysian note charging that Indonesian planes had violated Malaysian airspace 7 times between Nov. 13 and Dec. 8. The note also charged that regular Indonesian troops from Indonesian Borneo had attacked a Malaysian police post in Sabah Dec. 29. Malaysian Defense Min. Dato Abdul Razak bin Hussein said Dec. 31 that 9 Malaysian troops had been killed in the attack. The Malaysian government radio said 2 of the attackers were killed and one captured.

British Defense Min. Peter Thorneycroft held a series of defense meetings in Kuala Lumpur Jan. 5-6, 1964 with Malaysian Prime Min. Abdul Rahman and Defense Min. Dato Abdul Razak bin Hussein. A joint statement Jan. 6 said the British and Malaysians were "in full agreement on measures to be adopted" to "continue to meet Indonesian aggression."

Thorneycroft announced Jan. 10, after a tour of Sarawak, that British troops there had defeated nearly all terrorist bands that had crossed from Indonesian Borneo. In a clash there Jan. 7 British-led Gurkhas killed 3 Indonesian infiltrators and captured 4.

U.S. Arranges Cease-fire

A truce in the Indonesian-Malaysian border clashes was negotiated by U.S. Atty. Gen. Robert F. Kennedy at meetings Jan. 17-26, 1964 with leaders of Indonesia, Malaysia, Japan, the Philippines and Britain. The cease-fire went into effect Jan. 30.

Kennedy had left Washington Jan. 15 on a personal mission for Pres. Lyndon B. Johnson to seek a way to end the conflict. In addition to the truce, Kennedy arranged for the convening of a meeting in Bangkok, early in February, of foreign ministers of Indonesia, Malaysia and the Philippines as a possible preliminary to a 3-state summit conference to discuss Jakarta's and Manila's opposition to Malaysia.

Kennedy had met with Pres. Sukarno in Tokyo Jan. 17-18 and in Jakarta Jan. 22-23. Sukarno announced his agreement to the cease-fire after the later meeting. (Soon after Kennedy left Jakarta, Sukarno announced that Indonesia was still determined to "crush Malaysia," although Indonesia's "tactics may change." The U.S. State Department had confirmed Jan. 6 that Pres. Johnson had sent a note to Sukarno the previous week. Mr. Johnson reportedly warned that Jakarta's opposition to Malaysia was an obstacle to U.S.-Indonesian relations.)

Kennedy also conferred with Philippine Pres. Diosdado Macapagal in Manila Jan. 20, with Malaysian Premier Abdul Rahman in Kuala Lumpur Jan. 21 and with British Prime Min. Alec Douglas-Home in London Jan. 26-27.

Kennedy returned to Washington Jan. 28 and reported to Pres. Johnson. In a statement after the meeting, Kennedy said the only alternative to a peaceful solution of the Malaysian dispute was "continued war in the jungle." Kennedy warned that such a conflict "will escalate and very possibly involve other nations." He pointed out that the U.S. "has certain treaty obligations [the 1951 Anzus mutual defense pact signed by the U.S., Australia and New Zealand] and other certain responsibilities in that part of the world, so it is a very serious matter."

(Indonesian planes flew over the Malaysian-Indonesian border area Jan. 31 and dropped to Jakarta-backed guerrillas leaflets bearing an appeal from Sukarno to "stay where you are and safeguard your weapons." According to Malaysian sources, the pockets of infiltrators in Sarawak and Sabah consisted of about 150 Indonesian volunteers and some Sarawak Chinese Communists who had been trained in Indonesia.)

Bangkok Conferences Fail to End Dispute

The foreign ministers' conference arranged by U.S. Atty. Gen. Robert F. Kennedy was held in Bangkok, Thailand Feb. 5-10, 1964. The ministers — Subandrio of Indonesia, Salvador López of the Philippines and Tun Abdul Razak of Malaysia (also deputy prime minister) — agreed to have Thailand supervise the Malaysian-Indonesian truce. The ministers, however, failed to reach agreement on the status of the Indonesian-based guerrillas in Sarawak and Sabah. As a result, the proposed summit meeting of the 3 nations' top leaders had to be postponed pending another foreign ministers conference.

In agreeing on Thailand to supervise the cease-fire, the Bangkok conferees had requested UN Secy. Gen. U Thant's official appointment of their designee. In a reply Feb. 12, Thant said he had decided not to involve the UN in any role in the cease-fire. Thant said he would "limit" himself to noting that the 3 nations had appointed Thailand to supervise the truce.

The 3 foreign ministers met again in Bangkok Mar. 3-5 but again failed to reach agreement. As at the Feb. 5-10 meeting, the conference deadlock centered on the disposition of Indonesian guerrillas in Sarawak and Sabah. Subandrio of Indonesia rejected Malaysian demands that Indonesia withdraw about 400 pro-Indonesian guerrillas from Sabah and Sarawak. Malaysian Foreign Min. Tun Abdul Razak charged that the cease-fire negotiated in January by Robert Kennedy was being violated by Indonesia. The conferees agreed to send a Thai truce supervisory team to the fighting areas in Borneo.

The Malaysian cabinet had requested the 2d Bangkok conference in a note sent Feb. 24 to Thai Foreign Min. Thanat Khoman, who had acted as neutral chairman in the first foreign ministers' conference. The cabinet said the 2d meeting was necessary "in view of the rapidly deteriorating situation created by Indonesia."

The Malaysian cabinet's concern was reflected in reports of an increase in military activity on the Malaysian-Indonesian frontier: An Indonesian guerrilla unit crossed into Sarawak Feb. 20 and killed a Malaysian soldier in the Lundu district. 2 Malaysian policemen were killed and 6 wounded in a clash with Indonesian-based guerrillas in the Bau district of Sarawak Feb. 21. Charges of Indonesian cease-fire violations were made in notes sent Feb. 22 by the Malaysian government to Thai Foreign Min. Khoman, UN Secy. Gen. U Thant and U.S. Atty. Gen. Kennedy. The notes said the Feb. 21 clash had been the 6th such engagement between Indonesian guerrilla bands and Malaysian security forces since Jan. 30, the negotiated cease-fire date. A Sarawak security force Feb. 29 killed 4 Indonesian-based Chinese terrorists in a raid on their hiding place.

Malaysia informed Indonesia Feb. 23 that Sarawak and Sabah had been declared an air identification zone and that Indonesian planes found flying in the sector would be shot down. The warning was in reply to a statement by Indonesian

Foreign Min. Subandrio Feb. 22 that Jakarta planned to send food and other supplies to guerrillas in Sarawak and Sabah.

Sukarno Scorns U.S. Assistance

Sukarno, in a speech made Mar. 25, 1964, spurned U.S. economic aid. Speaking in Jakarta, Sukarno said: "To hell with your aid. We can do without aid. We'll never collapse. Indonesia is rich in natural resources. Indonesia is rich in manpower with its 103 million inhabitants — not like Malaysia with its 10 million."

Sukarno's remark about aid was an apparent reply to State Secy. Dean Rusk who had said Mar. 24 that Indonesia would receive no more U.S. aid until the Malaysia dispute was settled. U.S. assistance to Indonesia virtually ended with the arrival in Jakarta Mar. 26 of 40,000 tons of surplus rice. A U.S. Agency for International Development official said Washington had decided "not to give this government any aid that would directly support its current policies." Indonesia had asked the U.S. for all available surplus rice and an additional $56 million worth of surplus cotton.

Sukarno May 3 again scorned American aid. In a speech to 400,000 persons gathered in a park facing the U.S. embassy in Jakarta, Sukarno declared: "I said 'Go to hell with your aid,' and I meant the United States because there are circles in the United States who attached the condition to their aid that Indonesia stop its confrontation toward Malaysia."

Malaysia Charges Indonesian Expansionist Plot

A Malaysian government white paper charged Apr. 23, 1964 that Indonesian-supported subversive groups in Malaysia had planned to assassinate Malaysian Prime Min. Rahman, Deputy Prime Min. Razak and Singapore Prime Min. Lee Kuan Yew as part of a Jakarta government plot to crush Malaysia.

The white paper further charged that Indonesia was pursuing an expansionist policy to absorb Singapore and the Malay Peninsula into a "greater Indonesia." Sukarno, it said, sought to "create actively subversive, violent, communal, clandestine organizations within Malaysia." The white paper said 2 such organizations had been established in Aug. 1963, 2 weeks before the formation of Malaysia.

The white paper added: "Indonesian expansionism as a successor to Western imperialism and colonialism is a basic tenet of Sukarno's national policy. Indonesia's confrontation policy against Malaysia is the natural result of the long-term Indonesian policy and not the result of the formation of Malaysia, which is only an excuse made up by Indonesia to launch her present campaign of aggression."

Indonesian Defense Min. Abdul Haris Nasution confirmed May 2 that Indonesia was giving the anti-Malaysian guerrillas "concrete aid." Antara, Indonesia's official news agency, quoted Nasution as saying: "We are training them, and Pres. Sukarno has even ordered us to mobilize our volunteers to fight together with the North Kalimantan [Borneo] fighters to wipe out the British neo-colonialist plot."

Sukarno May 3 issued an "action command" requesting "21 million volunteers" "to help the peoples of Malaya, Singapore, Sarawak, Brunei and Sabah dissolve Malaysia and attain national independence." Charging that Malaysia "endangers the Indonesian revolution," Sukarno declared that his government had "endeavored to solve the issue through consultations" but "our endeavors have been met with humiliation and challenge."

Indonesia May 20 established its first volunteer combat brigade to be sent to the Sarawak and Sabah borders to be prepared "at any time" to join the anti-Malaysian "freedom fighters."

3-Nation Summit Meeting Fails

An effort to end the Malaysian-Indonesian dispute collapsed June 20, 1964 with an unsuccessful one-day conference in Tokyo of the heads of state of Malaysia, Indonesia and the Philippines.

The talks ended in deadlock when Malaysian Prime Min. Rahman and Pres. Sukarno failed to agree on a proposal by Philippine Pres. Macapagal that an Afro-Asian conciliation commission be established to "study" the dispute and recommend a solution. Rahman conditioned acceptance of the commission on the withdrawal of all Indonesian guerrillas from Sarawak and Sabah. Sukarno, opposing immediate withdrawal, insisted that the pull-back should await the commission's progress toward finding a political solution.

Rahman said on returning to Kuala Lumpur June 22 that the collapse of the Tokyo conference was due to Indonesia's failure to comply with the conditions for negotiations — withdrawal of its guerrillas.

Jakarta radio said June 21 that the failure of the conference impelled Indonesia to pursue its policy to crush Malaysia with greater vigor.

The summit talks had been arranged in Tokyo June 18 at a meeting of the foreign ministers of Indonesia, Malaysia and the Philippines. At the meeting, Malaysia revised its demand that all Indonesian guerrillas withdraw from Malaysian territory as its condition for attending a top-level conference. Malaysia, instead, accepted token withdrawal of part of Indonesia's 200 guerrillas. 32 of the guerrillas passed through a checkpoint at Tebedu in Sarawak June 19 in a token withdrawal verified by Thai observers.

Indonesian Guerrillas Resume Attacks, Land in Malaya

The collapse of the Tokyo summit conference signalled the resumption of Indonesian guerrilla attacks in Sarawak. The fighting intensified and spread as bands of Indonesian guerrillas landed on the Malaysian mainland state of Malaya in August-Sept. 1964.

About 100 Indonesian guerrillas fought a 6-hour battle June 21 with Malaysian security forces about 50 miles west of Kuching, Sarawak. 5 Gurkhas of the Malaysian forces were killed and 6 wounded. As a result of the clash, Malaysian security units in Sarawak were strengthened to counter insurgent raids. Malaysia had announced a nationwide draft June 4. The first phase provided for the immediate call-up of 12,000-15,000 men and women for military service and civil defense.

An Indonesian invasion force of about 40 men landed in Malaya Aug. 17. This was the first Indonesian attack on the Malaysian mainland. Malaysian authorities reported the immediate capture of 16 men. They reported Aug. 22 that 7 of the guerrillas had been killed; unofficial estimate of those captured was placed at 30-35. 2 Malaysian security soldiers were killed in mopping-up operations.

In a separate action Aug. 17, a Malaysian naval patrol intercepted and sank a small boat off the coast of Malaya's Johore state and captured 15 Indonesian guerrillas, according to the Malaysian radio.

Malaysia Aug. 17 protested to the UN Security Council against the Indonesian landings. The Indonesian Foreign Ministry said Aug. 18 that it had no knowledge of Malaya landings.

96 Indonesian guerrillas were parachuted from a U.S.-made C-130 Hercules transport the night of Sept. 1-2 into 2 areas near Labis in Johore state, about 85 miles south of Kuala Lumpur. By Sept. 21 at least 18 of the invaders were killed and 46 captured by Malaysian security forces. The Malaysians were aided by jet planes (Sept. 11-12) and by British-led Gurkhas and New Zealand troops. (Another New Zealand force conducted a search 65 miles from Labis for the remaining 40 survivors of an Indonesian guerrilla unit that had landed in the southwestern Pontian area Aug. 17.)

Indonesia'a armed forces were put on the alert Sept. 2 under an order issued by Pres. Sukarno to cope with alleged "enemy activities" that jeopardized "the safety of the nation." But the Indonesian Foreign Ministry denied Sept. 3 that an Indonesian parachute drop had taken place near Labis. It said that an Indonesian transport plane had flown over Singapore by mistake Sept. 2 but that the plane was carrying civilian dancers back to Cambodia and North Vietnam after performances in Indonesia.

Malaysia Sept. 4 issued a series of emergency regulations providing the death penalty for possessors of arms or explosives. In announcing the measures Sept. 3, Prime Min. Abdul Rahman had charged that Indonesia was preparing a "big offensive" against Malaysia with saboteurs and agents. Rahman charged Sept. 10 that at least 2,500 young Malaysians, mainly of Chinese ancestry, were being trained in Indonesia to fight against Malaysia as saboteurs and guerrilla fighters with the aid of Malaysian Communists. (Rahman reported these casualty totals in the guerrilla war in Sarawak and Sabah since Sept. 1963: 208 guerrillas killed, 205 captured, 83 wounded before escaping; 45 Malaysian and British troops killed, 60 wounded. The number of Indonesian guerrillas captured rose to 450 by early 1965.)

Indonesian Foreign Min. Subandrio announced Sept. 6 that his country would assume an "offensive attitude" in its drive to crush Malaysia. Following a meeting of the Supreme Operational Command, conducted by Sukarno, Subandrio said Indonesian forces "are now on the offensive to wipe out the enemy bases." Subandrio said Indonesia had "evidence" that foreign bases had been used for intrusions into Indonesian territory. He said 2 helicopters had recently been shot down over Indonesian Borneo.

Gen. Abdul Haris Nasution, Indonesia's armed forces chief, acknowledged Sept. 7 that "infiltrations of Malayan and Indonesian volunteers by sea and air have been going on for quite a long time into Malaya and North Borneo." Nasution said the Indonesian moves were in retaliation for the British shipment of arms and agents into the Indonesian states of Sumatra, Borneo and Celebes.

Britain stepped up measures to support its treaty commitment to defend Malaysia. A 500-man regiment from the British Army of the Rhine in West Germany was flown from Wildenrath Sept. 8, and the first planeload of troops arrived in Singapore Sept. 10.

The Malaysian government reported Oct. 27 that almost the entire Indonesian force that had landed in Malaya had been killed or captured. Of 108 who had landed at Pontian Aug. 17, 18 were reported killed and 72 captured. Of 96 who had landed in a parachute drop near Labis Sept. 2, 30 were killed and 60 captured. (It was reported that 53 Malaysians, mostly Chinese, were among the guerrillas involved.)

29 Indonesian paratroops, 20 Indonesian volunteers and 3 Malaysians landed from captured Malayan fishing boats at Muar on the southwest coast of Johore state Oct. 29. British, Australian, New Zealand and Malaysian forces were reported Nov. 1 to have captured all of the invaders and their arms.

A 28-man Indonesian force landed in the Pontian area Dec. 23; 24 of its members were reported captured and 3 killed by Dec. 27. The British frigate *Ajax* captured a party of 22 Indonesian guerrillas aboard 7 boats in the Strait of Malacca Dec. 24.

Malay-Chinese race riots had swept Singapore in July and again Sept. 4-12. 13 persons were killed, at least 87 injured and more than 150 arrested in the September riots. Prime

Min. Rahman said in a broadcast Sept. 4 that his régime had been warned that trouble would break out in Singapore simultaneously with guerrilla landings.

Soviet First Deputy Premier Anastas I. Mikoyan had disclosed at a rally in Jakarta June 25 that the Soviet Union was providing Indonesia with "very modern" weapons in the fight against Malaysia. Mikoyan had arrived in Indonesia June 22 and ended his visit July 3. The USSR July 17 pledged full support and more arms to aid Indonesia in its "crush Malaysia" policy. The pledge came at the conclusion of a one-week visit to Moscow by Indonesian Foreign Min. Subandrio and Lt. Gen. Achmad Yani, commander-in-chief of Indonesian ground forces.

U.S. State Undersecy. George W. Ball assured Malaysian Prime Min. Rahman as Rahman ended a visit to Washington July 24 that the U.S. would give strong support "not only to the concept of Malaysia but to its government in the difficulties it is now facing." Rahman said in New York July 31 that he had appealed to Pres. Johnson to intervene and persuade Soviet Premier Nikita S. Khrushchev to halt the flow of Soviet arms to Indonesia. He said he had requested U.S. arms aid at 2 White House meetings.

UN Meets on Malaysian Complaint

The UN Security Council met Sept. 9, 1964 to consider Malaysian charges of Indonesia's "blatant and inexcusable aggression." Malaysia had requested the Council meeting Sept. 3.

At the Council's opening session, Malaysian Home Affairs Min. Dr. Ismail bin Dato Abdul Rahman had submitted military equipment that he said had been captured with some of the Indonesian paratroopers. Indonesia's delegate, Deputy Foreign Min. Sudjarwo Tjondronegoro, referring to rebel activity in the Malaysian states of Sarawak and Sabah, said he could not deny that Indonesian guerrillas had joined the "militant youth" there in the fighting. He asked why Malaysia was "so greatly concerned" about the fighting spreading to Malaya. Tjondronegoro told the Council Sept. 14 that Indonesia was not fighting Malaysia but was attacking colonialism. He repeated Jakarta's frequent charges that Malaysia was a "neocolonialist" state created by Britain to encircle Indonesia and that this was the actual reason for the Indonesian-Malaysian dispute.

A Norwegian resolution deploring Indonesia's Sept. 1-2 air-drop of guerrillas in Malaya was favored by a 9-2 vote of the Council Sept. 17 but was defeated by a USSR veto. Voting for the resolution: the U.S., Britain, Bolivia, Brazil, Nationalist China, France, the Ivory Coast, Morocco and Norway. Against: the USSR and Czechoslovakia.

Among points of the resolution:

The Council regretted "all the incidents . . . in the whole region." Indonesia and Malaysia should "avoid occurrence of such incidents."

Both sides should abstain from threats or the use of force and respect each other's "territorial integrity and political independence" and attempt to revive bi-lateral negotiations. The talks should be resumed on the basis of a proposal for an Afro-Asian conciliation commission that had been made at the Malaysian-Indonesian meetings in Tokyo June 20.

Indonesia Quits UN

Indonesia withdrew from membership in the UN Jan. 1, 1965 in protest against the election of Malaysia to the UN Security Council. UN Secy. Gen. U Thant was formally informed of Jakarta's action when Indonesian Amb.-to-UN Lambertus N. Palar Jan. 21 handed him a note confirming the withdrawal. Indonesia thus became the first nation ever to leave the UN. Its resignation reduced the world body's membership to 114. (Indonesia rejoined the UN Sept. 28, 1966 after the Malaysian dispute was settled.)

Malaysia had been elected to a one-year term as a nonpermanent member of the Security Council Dec. 29, 1964 by the General Assembly. Malaysia assumed its Council seat Jan. 7.

Indonesia's opposition to Malaysia's candidacy for the Security Council had been expressed by Palar Dec. 29. In an interview in the N.Y. Times Jan. 4, Palar declared: "We want to make it clear to the world that we consider great harm has been done to us." Palar called Malaysia a "manifestation of British neocolonialism" and stressed that its election to the "highest security body in the world, an organization to guarantee the security of the new countries," was intolerable to Jakarta. He insisted that Malaysia's election to the Security Council was the sole reason for Indonesia's withdrawal from the UN.

Sukarno had warned in a speech in Jakarta Dec. 31, 1964 that Indonesia would leave the UN if Malaysia took the Security Council seat. Sukarno reaffirmed Indonesia's decision to quit the UN in another speech in Jakarta Jan. 7. He said: "In my announcement a few days ago I said that if Malaysia becomes a Security Council member I will order Indonesia to walk out of the United Nations. Now, since Malaysia has become a Security Council member, I declare that Indonesia has walked out of the United Nations." Emphasizing that his action meant Indonesia's "complete pull-out" from the UN, Sukarno added: "We can afford to operate without the United Nations specialized agencies. It is good for our nation to stand on our own feet. I have said: Go to hell with your aid." Sukarno repeated that "we will not have any more to do with the United Nations agencies."

Indonesian Foreign Min. Subandrio Jan. 12 ordered Vokjo P. Pavicic of Yugoslavia, the chief UN representative in Indonesia, to close his mission's offices and end all UN activities in the country.

In a cable to Sukarno Jan. 1, U Thant had expressed hope that Indonesia "would not think of withdrawing its cooperation" from the UN.

U.S. Amb.-to-UN Adlai E. Stevenson declared Jan. 2 that it was in "the manifest interest of the Indonesian people and of all peoples to preserve and improve the system of collective responsibility, to harmonize international relations and preserve the peace." He added: "No nation can profit in the long run from a lawless world of separate states, each pursuing its own sovereign ambitions. That way lies catastrophe."

Malaysian Prime Min. Abdul Rahman said Jan. 2 that Indonesia's withdrawal from the UN was "good riddance" and that "no one would shed any tears" over its departure.

Officials of the Japanese Foreign Ministry expressed fear Jan. 3 that Indonesia's withdrawal meant that it would join Peking to form a bloc in opposition to the "United States-Soviet collusion" that had preserved world peace.

U.S. officials Jan. 3 similarly suggested that Indonesia's action could lead to the emergence of a "Peking-Jakarta axis" for revolutionary movements. Sukarno's decision to leave the UN was believed to be principally linked to Indonesia's close ties with Communist China rather than the question of Malaysia's presence on the Security Council.

Many members of the UN's Afro-Asian bloc were reported Jan. 3 to have opposed Indonesia's action. An Indian delegate to the UN said that "any member going out of the United Nations is regrettable" and expressed hope that Indonesia would reconsider its departure. 11 African and Asian delegations were said to have appealed to Palar Jan. 6 to urge Sukarno to reverse himself.

Soviet Amb.-to-Indonesia Nikolai A. Mikhailov visited Foreign Min. Subandrio in Jakarta Jan. 5 and reportedly expressed Moscow's opposition to Indonesia's action on the ground that it merely would add to Southeast Asian tensions.

Communist Chinese Amb.-to-Indonesia Yao Chung-ming visited Subandrio Jan. 6 and was reported to have communicated Peking's strong endorsement of Indonesia's action. The Chinese Communist Party newspaper *Jenmin Jih Pao (People's Daily)* Jan. 6 called the UN "a vile place [intended] for a few powers to share the spoils"; Indonesia, it said, "has truly asserted its independence and sovereignty."

Malaysia Warns Jakarta Against Raids

The Malaysian government declared Jan. 4, 1965 that it was "prepared to take retaliatory action under the rule of hot pursuit" if its territory were subjected to new Indonesian guerrilla attacks. The announcement was made by Prime Min. Abdul Rahman following an emergency cabinet session in Kuala Lumpur. Rahman said the cabinet also had decided: "to inform the UN of the seriousness of the threat of more intensive Indonesian attacks and to request the UN to assist us in the defense of our nation in the event of such a happening"; "to ask our allies under the defense agreement to review the latest position and send reinforcements, if necessary"; "to expedite the expansion of our own forces by establishing more training centers."

In continuing British moves to reinforce its Malaysian garrison, 70 British paratroopers were flown to Singapore Jan. 8, and the aircraft carrier *Eagle* arrived at the Singapore naval base Jan. 13. British Prime Min. Harold Wilson had said Jan. 7 that British forces in Malaysia totaled 50,000 men.

A Malaysian protest note delivered to UN Security Council Pres. Liu Chieh of Nationalist China Jan. 7 charged that Indonesia was building up its military forces opposite Sarawak and Sabah as part of a possible move to carry out Jakarta's avowed plan to crush Malaysia.

Sukarno denied Jan. 13 that Indonesia was preparing for war against Malaysia. Interviewed in Jakarta by CBS-TV, Sukarno said that "if Indonesia is attacked, the Indonesian people will fight back, but Indonesia will never begin the fighting." Sukarno asserted that the crisis could be solved if Malaysia carried out the 1963 Manila agreements for UN surveys to determine whether the peoples of Sarawak and Sabah wanted to be part of Malaysia.

Despite Sukarno's denials of aggressive intentions against Malaysia, Indonesian infiltrators launched new attacks. An Indonesian guerrilla force of 24 men landed Jan. 8 at Tanjong Piai, in southern Malaya. 13 of the guerrillas were rounded up by Malaysian forces by Jan. 9. An Indonesian tug carrying 40 raiders was sunk by a Malaysian patrol ship Jan. 9 in the Malacca Straits. 12 of the raiders were picked up immediately, and 12 others were reported captured the same day after landing at Kota Tinggi, 180 miles south of Kuala Lumpur.

Malaysian police Jan. 27 arrested 4 men on charges of planning an armed revolt in Malaysia with Indonesian aid. Among those seized were Raja Hinifah, a leader of the opposition rightwing Pan-Malayan Islamic Party, and Kampo Radjo, a leader of the opposition leftwing National Convention Party. Malaysian police Jan. 29 arrested ex-Agriculture Min. Abdul Aziz bin Ishak and Burhanuddin al-Hemi, president of the Pan-Malayan Islamic Party. They were accused of planning to set up an Indonesian-backed Malaysian government in exile.

The Malaysian government announced Mar. 15 that Malaysian security forces had killed or captured 29 Indonesian commandos who had landed Feb. 25 in the Kota Tinggi coastal area of Johore state. The Malaysian Defense Ministry had reported Mar. 3 that 8 Malaysian security force members had been killed and 5 wounded in a jungle ambush by the Indonesian commandos. Malaysian authorities Mar. 6 instituted a curfew for 100 miles of coastline facing Indonesia.

Solutions Sought

Sukarno Jan. 14, 1965 proposed another UN poll of Sarawak and Sabah to determine whether their inhabitants wanted to remain part of the Malaysian Federation. Asserting that this was the only way to solve the Indonesian-Malaysian dispute, Sukarno told Western correspondents in Jakarta that he would "abide by" the results despite Indonesia's withdrawal from the UN. "Am I not a man of peace?" he asked. If the UN refused to conduct such a poll, Sukarno said, Indonesia would favor an investigation of the dispute by an Afro-Asian conciliation commission.

The Malaysian Foreign Ministry replied Jan. 15: Following "abortive peace talks with Indonesia, Malaysia . . . would rather see a genuine demonstration of the professed desire rather than hear mere expressions of it"; Malaysia would cooperate with any Afro-Asian conciliation commission but only after "Indonesia ceased hostilities and all acts of aggression and is ready to respect Malaysia's sovereignty and territorial integrity."

Indonesian Foreign Min. Subandrio declared Feb. 8 that Indonesia "has always been willing to negotiate." He suggested that negotiations be held under these terms: (a) Malaysia would first be disbanded and its components — Malaya, Singapore, Sabah and Sarawak — would become independent states; (b) these states could join Indonesia and the Philippines in a loose confederation to be called Maphilindo.

Malaysia Prime Min. Rahman agreed Apr. 20, following a 2-hour meeting in Kuala Lumpur with Japanese special envoy Shojiro Kawashima, to accept a Japanese proposal to meet with Sukarno again in an effort to end the Malaysian-Indonesian conflict. But Sukarno declared at a May Day celebration in Jakarta May 1 that he had refused the offer for peace talks in Tokyo. Sukarno asserted: "Our tactics may change 24 times in one day as long as our goal is the same. We will not cease until we have pulverized this neocolonialist project."

Indonesia Launches Anti-U.S. Drive

Angered at U.S. support of Malaysia in its dispute with Indonesia, the Jakarta government carried out a series of harassing moves and punitive measures against U.S. business interests and American officials in Indonesia during 1965.

U.S. Information Agency Director Carl T. Rowan announced Mar. 4 that his agency was discontinuing its operations in Indonesia and was "most reluctantly" closing its 5 libraries and reading rooms there. He said harassment by the Indonesian government "has left us no choice." He charged: "Not only has it [the Indonesian government] failed to restrain those who have attacked the libraries periodically, but it has now seized the libraries and placed the whole USIA operation under conditions that we find intolerable. Until such time as our libraries and personnel can function under conditions that meet an acceptable standard of international conduct, USIA will cease to operate in Indonesia."

A Jakarta apartment building housing employees of the U.S. embassy was deprived of its gas and electricity Mar. 18 by Communist labor unions. The utility workers also cut off electricity at the Jakarta offices of the Indonesian-American Friendship Society, an activity sponsored by the U.S. embassy, and at the Associated Press offices. U.S. Amb. Howard P. Jones lodged a protest with the Jakarta régime, and service was restored Mar. 23. The Communist unions said they had shut off the gas and electricity in retaliation for the U.S.' decision to grant Malaysia a $4 million arms credit. (Malaysian Deputy Premier-Defense Min. Abdul Razak and U.S. Amb.-to-Malaysia James D. Bell had signed the $4-million arms pact Mar. 7.)

Indonesia's Communist-run postal workers' union Mar. 23 imposed a mail and telegraph boycott on the U.S. embassy. The union also refused to handle outgoing dispatches of the AP and UPI and incoming *N.Y. Times* messages. The embassy had direct communications with Washington and received its mail by diplomatic pouch, and these services were uninterrupted. But the boycott prevented the embassy from receiving internal mail and telegrams. The embassy protested the boycott.

The Indonesian government Mar. 19 had seized 3 U.S.-owned oil companies: Stanvac (jointly owned by the Standard Oil Co. [New Jersey] and the Socony Mobil Oil Co.); Caltex (owned by the Standard Oil Co. of California and Texaco, Inc.); Pan American Oil. A 4th oil company, Shell Oil, a member of the Dutch-British-owned Royal Dutch Shell Group, also was seized. Sukarno announced the seizures after a meeting with Basic Industries & Mining Min. Chaerul Saleh. Saleh had submitted to Sukarno a petition he had received earlier that day from 1,000 Communist-led workers, who demanded government possession of the companies.

The Indonesian government Mar. 23 seized a Goodyear Tire factory at Bogor, about 35 miles south of Jakarta. The assets of the American-owned plant were estimated at $5 million. 2 more U.S.-owned firms were seized by the Indonesian government the following month — the National Cash Register Co. (reported Apr. 2) and the National Carbon Co. (reported Apr. 15).

Deteriorating U.S.-Indonesian relations were discussed in Jakarta Mar. 31-Apr. 14 by Sukarno and ex-U.S. Amb. Ellsworth Bunker, Pres. Johnson's personal emissary. The 2 announced in a joint communiqué issued at the end of the talks Apr. 14 that the U.S. would withdraw its Peace Corps from Indonesia. The Bunker-Sukarno communiqué conceded that the Malaysian problem was partially responsible for U.S.-Indonesian differences. (A statement issued by Peace Corps director Sargent Shriver Apr. 14 said Indonesia had not questioned "the volunteers' effectiveness or their fidelity to their work or the warm relationships they have established with the Indonesian peoples." "The larger issues of world politics have supervened," Shriver said. The Indonesian Communist Party had been campaigning to get the corps out of Indonesia.)

Indonesia Opposes British Base in Singapore

Singapore's withdrawal from the Malaysian Federation Aug. 9, 1965 brought Indonesia into further conflict with Britain. Singapore, whose 1,820,000 residents were mostly Chinese, decided to withdraw because of the federation's domination by Malays. Under one of the provisions of an Independence of Singapore Agreement, signed Aug. 7 by Malaysian Prime Min. Abdul Rahman and Singapore Prime Min. Lee Kuan Yew, Britain was to retain its military and naval base in Singapore. Denouncing Lee's decision to permit Britain to maintain a military foothold in Singapore, Indonesian Defense Min. Abdul Haris Nasution warned Aug. 11 that Indonesia would seek to crush the base. Nasution added, however, that "things will be different if Lee is willing to remove it."

An Indonesian Foreign Ministry spokesman Aug. 9 had called Singapore's departure from the Malaysian Federation "a complete defeat of the British policy artifically to create the Malaysian Federation as a base for subversion against Indonesia." Indonesian Foreign Min. Subandrio asserted Aug. 9 that his government's policy of "confrontation will continue until Malaysia has been completely destroyed." (Subandrio was ousted from the government in a drastic shake-up in Mar. 1966. Adam Malik, his successor as foreign minister, said Apr. 10, 1966 that Sukarno had instructed him to seek to establish relations with Singapore in an apparent move to widen the split between Singapore and Malaysia.)

Indonesian-Malaysian Dispute Settled

Indonesia and Malaysia resumed diplomatic efforts to settle their dispute at a ministerial conference in Bangkok May 29, 1966 after Indonesian internal up-heavals had resulted in an almost total erosion of Sukarno's power. Indonesian-Malaysian agreement was reached June 1, and a pact ending Indonesia's "confrontation with Malaysia" was signed in Jakarta Aug. 11. (The Bangkok conference followed an offer by Malaysian Prime Min. Rahman Apr. 16 to hold peace talks if Indonesia called off its guerrilla war against Malaysia.)

The bi-lateral accord was signed by the 2 ministers who had negotiated the agreement in Bangkok—Indonesian Foreign Min. Adam Malik and Malaysian Deputy Prime Min. Abdul Razak.

The treaty provided for the immediate restoration of diplomatic relations between Indonesia and Malaysia, an exchange of diplomatic representatives and a cessation of the undeclared hostilities on their borders. The pact also sought to remove the principal stumbling block to peaceful Indonesian-Malaysian ties — the disposition of the Malaysian states of Sabah and Sarawak. Malaysia agreed to hold a public referendum in the 2 states to determine whether their inhabitants preferred to remain in the federation.

In its first normalization action, Malaysia announced Aug. 13 the removal of the nighttime curfew on the southeast and southwest coasts of West Malaysia.

Sukarno at first had opposed the Bangkok peace talks, according to a statement made by Foreign Min. Malik May 20. Malik said that Sukarno, in an apparent effort to block the meeting, had forbidden him to leave the country. (Charging that the policy of opposing Malaysia had injured Indonesia's economy, Malik said at a Jakarta rally of students that "the confrontation of the people's stomachs is more important than any other confrontation.") Jakarta radio reported May 23 that Sukarno had reversed his position and approved the Indonesian-Malaysian talks.

Lt. Gen. Suharto, who had taken over most of Sukarno's powers, had declared Apr. 9 that Indonesia would continue its policy of confrontation against the Federation of Malaysia. But he said Jakarta did not rule out the possibility of establishing peaceful relations with Malaysia. Suharto said the purpose of the confrontation policy was "to struggle for the rights of those people [in Malaysia] for democratic self-determination." Suharto said Indonesia would accept Malaysia's existence if it could be proven that citizens of the Malaysian states of Sarawak and Sabah wanted to remain in the federation. Suharto accused Britain of supporting Malaysia as a pretext for keeping troops in Southeast Asia. The British presence there, he said, was "an anachronism that no longer accords with the awakening of Asia." The pro-army newspaper *Triskati* had said Apr. 7: "A peaceful confrontation" was preferrable to the "physical confrontation, or war, that was inspired by the Indonesian Communist Party for the interests of China. Within the framework of a peaceful confrontation we could become the mediator in the dispute between Malaysia and North Borneo, thereby giving an example of how Asians solve specific Asian problems."

Indonesia's Crush Malaysia Command was formally disbanded Aug. 22. The command had been created by Sukarno

Feb. 22 to carry out military operations in Indonesia's policy of confrontation with Malaysia. The command was succeeded by the body it had originally replaced—the Supreme Operations Command.

SUKARNO'S DOWNFALL

1965-67

During 1965-67 Indonesia suffered its most critical upheaval since it became an independent country in 1945. This period was marked by an unsuccessful coup, the violent suppression of the Indonesian Communist Party (PKI) and its followers in retaliation for the PKI's alleged involvement in the abortive uprising and an erosion of Pres. Sukarno's powers followed by his total political downfall. Sukarno's domestic fall took place after it became evident that he no longer had any chance of success in what some observers considered a grandiose ambition to lead a coalition of "neutralist" nations that could play off West against East and wield decisive power in world affairs.

Although the attempted coup, launched Sept. 30, 1965, was first reported to be a plot to overthrow Sukarno, the president was later accused of having been involved with the PKI in engineering it. The charges, raised by the army, came at a time of growing public discontent with Sukarno's 20-year rule.

An army drive to curb Sukarno began Mar. 12, 1966, when Sukarno was forced to cede political powers to Lt. Gen. Suharto, army commander, who emerged as Indonesia's new strongman. A series of other restrictive measures instituted against Sukarno culminated in action in which the Provisional People's Consultative Congress Mar. 7, 1967 deprived Sukarno of all ceremonial powers and stripped him of all titles.

The suppression of the PKI constituted one of the bloodiest chapters in Indonesia's recent history of almost continual violence. The anti-Communist drive was carried out by organized armed forces attacks and by indiscriminate vengeful raids by Moslem mobs. The death toll was believed to have been high, although a precise count was never made available. Sukarno reported Jan. 15, 1966 that a government fact-finding mission had estimated that 87,000 persons had been killed. All but a few of the dead were reported to have been Communists or Communist sympathizers. The *N.Y. Times* reported Jan. 12 that more than 100,000 Communists and their sympathizers had been slain by village vigilante groups composed of devout Moslems. The *Times'* death toll figure was confirmed Sept. 11 by Indonesian Amb.-to-U.S. Lambertus N. Palar. Asserting that not all of those slain were Communists, Palar said many of those killed were victims of "village quarrels."

Rebellion Crushed

Indonesian army rebels Sept. 30, 1965 had launched what appeared to be an armed attempt to overthrow Pres. Sukarno. The rebels, calling themselves the "30th of September Movement," captured the government radio station and other strategic points in Jakarta but were quickly surrounded and defeated by forces supporting the Sukarno government. The government charged that the abortive coup had received support from the PKI (the Indonesian Communist Party), although this was never conclusively proven. The rebel forces were headed by Lt. Col. Untung, a battalion commander in Sukarno's personal bodyguard. Other rebel leaders were Col. Suherman, commander of the Diponegoro Division, which had joined the rebels, Brig. Gen. Supardjo and Col. A. Latief, 1st Infantry Brigade commander. Latief was seized Oct. 9, and Untung was reported Oct. 11 to have been captured.

After capturing the government radio station, the insurgents announced in a broadcast that they had formed a Revolutionary Council and a 45-member cabinet. The broadcast said that Untung had acted to prevent an anti-Sukarno *coup d'état* planned for Oct. 5. The broadcast said: The anti-Sukarno coup was planned by a "council of generals" "sponsored" by the U.S.' CIA (Central Intelligence Agency). The pro-U.S. council had been "very active lately, especially after Pres. Sukarno was seriously ill in the first week of August. Their hope that Pres. Sukarno would die of his illness did not materialize."

Denying that an anti-Sukarno coup had been planned for Oct. 5, the Indonesian government charged that Untung's action was aimed at outright seizure of power.

The U.S. denied Oct. 1 that the CIA was involved in the Indonesian revolt. (Indonesia's Antara news agency had asserted Sept. 24 that 10 CIA agents had been arrested at Menado in North Celebes after being smuggled into the Indonesian island from the Philippines. A U.S. embassy spokesman in Jakarta Sept. 25 denied the allegation.)

The rebel radio reported that members of the 45-member insurgent cabinet included First Deputy Premier and Foreign Min. Subandrio, 2d Deputy Premier Johannes Leimena, Vice Adm. R. E. Martadinata, the navy commander, and Vice Marshal Omar Dhani, air force commander. Jakarta radio reported Oct. 3 that Dhani had disavowed support of the rebels and that the air force had not been involved in the uprising.

After announcing the seizure of power Sept. 30, the rebel radio went off the air. 5 hours later the station resumed broadcasting with a government announcement Oct. 1 that the coup had been crushed and that Jakarta was in the hands of loyal soldiers. Sporadic fighting continued elsewhere in Central Java, however.

Sukarno announced over Jakarta radio Oct. 2 that he was still "carrying out the leadership of the state and government" and that he retained control of the army leadership. He announced that he had appointed Gen. Suharto as temporary army chief to replace Gen. Abdul Haris Nasution. Nasution, who was also defense minister, had been injured in escaping a rebel kidnap attempt at the start of the revolt. (Nasution's 5-year-old daughter, shot during the abduction attempt, died of her wounds Oct. 6.) Suharto commanded elements of the pro-government Siliwangi Division, which had recaptured the government radio station in Jakarta Oct. 2.

Lt. Gen. Achmad Yani, army chief of staff, and 5 other army generals who had been kidnaped by rebels at the start of the coup were found dead Oct. 4 in a common grave near the Halim air base outside Jakarta. Brig. Gen. Supardjo reportedly had commanded the troops who had engineered the abduction and slayings. Suharto blamed the slayings on Vice Marshal Dhani and the air force. Dhani had acknowledged the involvement of some air force elements in the abortive coup although earlier Oct. 4 Sukarno had absolved the air force of any participation in the uprising. (Shortly after the revolt was crushed, Dhani was sent out of the country on a mission for the government. But he was brought back later to stand trial in 1966.) The army charged that Communist youth members and officials of the PKI-operated Sobsi Labor Federation had been involved in the executions. An army newspaper announced Oct. 8 that 3 Communist youths had been arrested and had confessed to participating in the murders. Jakarta radio reported Oct. 9 that a 7th general, identified as Brig. Gen. Samusi of the National Police, had been slain by the rebels Oct. 1.

The government reported Oct. 6 the capture of the last rebel stronghold in Jogjakarta, 250 miles southeast of Jakarta. The announcement said the Diponegoro Division had rejoined the government side and was instrumental in the defeat of the rebels in the city. The broadcast said other pro-government army troops had captured about 2,000 members of Communist paramilitary units in other actions in crushing the revolt. The government said the rebels had killed at least 72 relatives of government soldiers fighting insurgent remnants in Central Java.

Subandrio reported Oct. 7 that order had been fully restored in Central Java. An Indonesian broadcast said that 70 government soldiers had been killed in the fighting there and that 60 were missing.

The army reported Oct. 12 that government troops had found evidence of Chinese Communist arms furnished to the rebels. The evidence was turned up in a raid on a Communist stronghold at Bekasi, 15 miles east of Jakarta.

Army Launches Anti-Communist Drive

The Indonesian army began widespread arrests of members of the PKI in early Oct. 1965 on the charge that the party had supported the abortive coup. The PKI and its installations in Jakarta and other cities were attacked by Moslem and Christian demonstrators demanding the party's dissolution. By Oct. 10 army sources estimated that more than 1,000 Communists and leftists had been seized.

The PKI Oct. 7 denied Communist involvement in the coup. A party statement called the uprising "an internal affair of the army." It insisted that the Communists who had been listed in a rebel Revolutionary Council at the start of the coup had been named without their approval.

At a cabinet meeting Oct. 6, Sukarno expressed opposition to the army's campaign against the Communists. (Sukarno was reported to have encouraged the growth of the PKI to offset the influence of the army.) Jakarta radio announced Oct. 11 that Sukarno had later reversed his position and supported the anti-Communist drive.

Sukarno Oct. 14 appointed Maj. Gen. Suharto to replace leftist Maj. Gen. Pranoto Reksosamudro as commander of the army. Sukarno had appointed Pranoto to the post immediately after the abortive coup. Suharto was installed as commander Oct. 16.

The army Oct. 18 temporarily prohibited the activities of the PKI and its affiliated groups in the Jakarta area. This restriction on the PKI was extended to Central Java and South Sumatra Oct. 23. Among the organizations affected were Permuda Rakjat, the youth wing, and the Sobsi Labor Federation. The PKI ban followed an army order Oct. 16 that had outlawed activities by all political groups reputedly involved in the coup.

Sukarno Oct. 16 extended the "state of war," in effect throughout the country since the start of the coup. The extension gave the army stricter control over several government operations normally under civilian jurisdiction. The decree continued military control of newspapers and radio stations. The army had banned Communist newspapers.

The cabinet's presidium Oct. 22 promulgated these measures to restrict the PKI: All government ministers were ordered to suspend any PKI-affiliated organizations under their control; cabinet ministers were directed to temporarily dismiss subordinates suspected of being involved in the 30th of September Movement and to dishonorably discharge aides whose links with the movement were proven.

The army expanded its drive against the PKI by declaring martial law in Central Java Oct. 28. The army acted after it had reported Oct. 27 that Communists had killed 178 persons in eastern and Central Java since the crushing of the attempted coup.

Anti-Red Drive Intensifies

Deputy Premier Chaerul Saleh reported Oct. 30, 1965 that PKI armed forces in Central Java had stepped up military attacks on government soldiers and anti-Communist elements and that the fighting had assumed aspects of a full-fledged revolt. The clashes coincided with an intensification of public demonstrations against the PKI, demands for the party's dissolution and further government restrictions against the PKI.

Among military and political developments in late October and November:

■ The Antara news agency reported Oct. 30 that government soldiers had killed 50 Communist youths in a clash in Prambanan. In another engagement, army paratroopers threw back a Communist armed attempt to encircle Klaten and captured 72 prisoners, Antara reported.

■ Jakarta radio disclosed Oct. 30 that government paratroopers had captured 342 rebels, all members of the PKI Worker Front. 38 other rebels were said to have been killed in an attempt to ambush a navy patrol in the Surakarta District.

■ Antara Oct. 31 quoted army sources as saying that PKI rebels Oct. 29 had seized the 2 district regions of Djatimo and Manisrenggo, near Jogjakarta. Government troops encountered strong resistance in attempting to recapture the 2 districts. The army charged that the rebels had slain 25 members of Moslem and Nationalist groups in Manisrenggo and had kidnaped 82 others.

■ Fighting was reported Nov. 2 to have spread to eastern and western Java. 500 PKI youth-wing members battled government troops, reinforced by paramilitary units, in the eastern end of the island in the Kediri-Madiun region. Communist unrest also was reported in Surabaya, where 50 PKI waterfront-union members were seized on charges of pro-rebel activity.

■ The army extended its military control Nov. 3 by taking over the civilian intelligence agency, which had been headed by First Deputy Premier Subandrio. The decision was announced by Gen. Suharto as he presented his new military high command to Sukarno. Subandrio had been under sharp attack since the coup. The army had charged that he had tried to link the U.S.' CIA with the alleged plot of the council of generals to overthrow Sukarno. Moslem and student groups had assailed Subandrio for opposition to the army's anti-PKI campaign.

■ Jakarta radio announced Nov. 2 that 57 PKI and leftwing members of the House of Representatives had been suspended for alleged involvement in the anti-Sukarno coup. Jakarta radio also announced that other PKI members and leftists were being ousted from posts in courts and the defense and security departments.

■ Agrarian Affairs Min. Hermanses Nov. 4 announced the suspension of all National Land Reform Committee members who had been linked with the PKI-affiliated Indonesian Peasant Front. The move was made to counter a PKI drive to convince peasants that only the PKI would bring about land reform, Hermanses said.

■ Sukarno Nov. 6 pledged "appropriate action" against the PKI. Addressing the cabinet at Bogor, Sukarno called the uprising "disgraceful" but said efforts of rightwing reactionaries to exploit the revolt for their own advantage were "more dangerous than the revolt itself." Sukarno said that the U.S. had offered him a bribe of 150 million Indonesian rupiahs if he would introduce "free-world ideologies" into Indonesia. Sukarno said that several days after the revolt had been suppressed, U.S. officials in Indonesia, who had been "anti-Sukarno and anti-Indonesia," "changed their tune." "They were happy to know I was against this rebel movement." Sukarno said he had been approached by U.S. Amb. Marshal Green, and he quoted Green as having said: "We love Indonesia—we want to help Indonesia." Despite the U.S.' professions of sympathy, Sukarno claimed, the U.S. supported West Java's rightwing Darul Islam movement, a Moslem group that opposed his government.

■ Maj. Gen. Ibrahim Adije, military commander in West Java, announced Nov. 19 that he had imposed a total ban on the PKI in that region. Similar action against the PKI was taken by military commanders in the Jakarta military area, South Celebes, the Moluccas and West Borneo.

■ Col. Harsono, chief of press and public relations in the Information Ministry, reported Dec. 5 that 46 of Indonesia's 163 newspapers had been shut because of alleged PKI ties or because of failure to obey new press laws. Harsono said that the number of newspapers would eventually be reduced to a total of about 65. The sharp reduction was designed to conform with a government ruling that stipulated the operation of only one daily newspaper for each of the 8 remaining political parties and one each for several organizations and government agencies.

Sukarno Forms Triumvirate

Sukarno Dec. 14, 1965 transformed the Supreme Operational Command into a triumvirate that was to rule as an executive body under him. Gen. Suharto said that as a result of the shift, Deputy Premier-Foreign Min. Subandrio had been removed as deputy commander of the Operational Command.

The command's 3 deputy commanders were Gen. Abdul Haris Nasution, defense minister, Sultan Hamengku Buwono, governor of the Jogjakarta district and defense minister in the early 1950s, and Information Min. Ruslan Abdulgani, who had been replaced as foreign minister by Subandrio. Nasution was to handle military matters. Buwono was to deal with economic and general matters, and Abdulgani's area was to be social and political affairs.

Sukarno Nov. 27 removed Air Vice Marshal Omar Dhani as air force commander and appointed Air Vice Marshal Sri Muljono Herlambang in his place. Herlambang was Dhani's deputy. Dhani was named minister of aviation, a post with little power.

Army Hunts for PKI Leader Aidit

PKI Secy. Gen. Dipa Nusantara Aidit, 43, a minister without portfolio in Sukarno's cabinet, was a prime target in the army's search for Communists. Aidit disappeared one day before the outbreak of the coup. Unofficial accounts of his whereabouts, all contradictory, were reported from time to time, but his fate remained a mystery.

The first report on Aidit appeared Oct. 12 in a Hong Kong newspaper, which said that he had fled Sept. 29 from Jakarta to the Javanese fishing port of Tunban (360 miles east of Jakarta) and then had been picked up by a Communist Chinese submarine. At his last public appearance, in Jakarta

Sept. 28, Aidit had called on his followers at a Communist youth rally to destroy Ansor, the Moslem youth movement. Aidit had criticized Sukarno in his presence and had accused army leaders of squandering public funds.

The Jakarta correspondent of the Tokyo newspaper *Asahi Shimbun* reported Nov. 29 that Aidit had been shot to death while trying to escape from a prison Nov. 22 near Surakarta in Central Java.

Jakarta sources reported Dec. 1 that Aidit had been shot and killed Nov. 22 by army units that had been searching for him.

A report from Singapore Dec. 6 said Aidit was alive under Indonesian army guard.

Another high-ranking PKI leader, Njono bin Sastroedjo, 43, was captured Oct. 2. Njono was described as the 7th ranking member of the PKI's Central Committee.

Relations With Communist China Deteriorate

Indonesian charges linking Communist China with the attempted coup against Sukarno, coupled with the resulting campaign against the PKI, led to a sharp deterioration in Jakarta-Peking relations during 1965.

A Peking protest note to Indonesia Oct. 18 charged that 40 Indonesian troops had forced their way into Communist China's Commercial Center in Jakarta Oct. 16, had opened fire, had ransacked the offices and had manhandled staff members. The note demanded an apology and punishment of those responsible. Peking complained that "since Oct. 1 lies and slanders" about China's alleged rôle in the abortive coup and "anti-Chinese clamors have continuously appeared in Indonesia and all kinds of threats have been made against the Chinese diplomatic mission."

Indonesian 2d Deputy Foreign Min. Ganis Harsono Oct. 19 conceded that Indonesian soldiers might have entered the building while searches were being made as part of an effort to crush any remaining rebel activity.

China's first published account of the coup, published Oct. 20 by the official news agency Hsinhua, assailed right-wing army generals for imposing an "atmosphere of terror" in Indonesia. The statement denounced the drive against the PKI and charged that the anti-Chinese incidents were army-inspired.

Hsinhua reported Oct. 23 that an Indonesian soldier and 2 policemen had "forced their way into" the Chinese embassy's living quarters in Jakarta Oct. 21. The embassy, protesting to Indonesia, demanded an apology and punishment of the perpetrators of "this fresh violation of its diplomatic privileges."

Sukarno conferred Oct. 26 with Chinese Amb. Yao Chung-ming. After the talks, a Chinese embassy official said "the relations between China and Indonesia remain firm although there are elements trying to alienate China and Indonesia."

A mob of about 100,000 Indonesian demonstrators attacked the Communist Chinese consulate in Medan, North Sumatra Nov. 2 in protest against Peking's alleged involvement in the coup. The rioters tore down a Chinese flag and destroyed an emblem on the building. A protest note, reported Nov. 5 to have been delivered by the Chinese embassy in Jakarta to the Indonesian government, demanded a public apology for this "extremely serious provocation."

Hsinhua charged Nov. 6 that anti-Communist activity in Indonesia threatened the "overseas Chinese" there. Hsinhua said that despite appeals by Chinese diplomats, "violent victimization of overseas Chinese has not ceased, and there are even signs of its spreading and growing in intensity."

Despite strained Sino-Indonesian relations, Sukarno announced Nov. 20 that "in our struggle against imperialism we continue to exist in the Jakarta-Pnompenh-Hanoi-Peking-Pyongyang axis."(Sukarno had first publicly proclaimed the adherence of Indonesia to the "anti-imperialist axis" of Communist China, North Vietnam, North Korea and Cambodia in an Indonesian Independence Day speech Aug. 17.)

Foreign Min. Subandrio confirmed Dec. 3 that relations between Indonesia and Communist China "have become strained lately." In an interview in the army newspaper, *Berit Yudha (War News)*, Subandrio said: "this is because the public feels that China is, if not responsible, at least sympathetic toward the 30th of September Movement." Subandrio said Jakarta wanted friendly relations with Peking because they both opposed neocolonial imperialism. "But let us respect each other and not interfere with each other's internal differences," he added.

The Chinese Communist consulate in Medan, North Sumatra was attacked again Dec. 10 by about 2,000 Indonesian demonstrators. 3 persons were reported killed. After the attack, the mob roamed through the city and raided the homes and stores of ethnic Chinese. A Chinese protest note to the Jakarta government Dec. 16 said 3 consulate staff members had been injured by brick-throwing demonstrators. Another Chinese note Dec. 19 charged that the Dec. 10 riots against the Chinese community in Medan had spread to other parts of North Sumatra.

Cabinet Reorganized, Nasution Ousted

Sukarno Feb. 21, 1966 dismissed Gen. Abdul Haris Nasution, 47, as defense minister and chief of the armed forces. Nasution was ousted in a major cabinet reorganization aimed at halting or slowing the anti-Communist campaign that followed the abortive 1965 coup. 14 other anti-Communist military ministers also were relieved of their posts. Nasution's armed forces post was abolished. Maj. Gen. Haji Sarbini, veterans affairs minister, replaced Nasution as defense minister. Vice Adm. Eddie Mertadinata, a Nasution supporter, was replaced by Vice Adm. Mulaydi as navy commander. Kiai Haji Ídham Chalid, chairman of the Moslem Religious Teachers Party, was appointed 4th deputy premier.

No official reasons were given for Nasution's ouster. He had spearheaded the army drive against the PKI since the abortive coup and had emerged as a powerful figure with strong anti-Communist support. His dismissal triggered widespread anti-Communist and anti-government demonstrations in Jakarta. Several hundred pro-Nasution students attempted to storm the Presidential Palace in Jakarta Feb. 23 and 24 but were stopped by police. 3 students were killed and several wounded in the 2d demonstration.

Speaking in Jakarta Feb. 28 at a student rally sponsored by the Nationalist Party, Sukarno declared: "Our revolution will soon return to its original leftist rails. The recent moves to turn our revolution to the right will fail."

A Jakarta broadcast Feb. 28 quoted Gen. Nasution as urging all Indonesians to "defend the unity of the armed forces, the masses and the great leader of the revolution, Pres. Sukarno." Nasution assailed certain unidentified groups whom he said were waging "political guerrilla warfare" by "trying to divert us from wiping out the Communist Party."

Students intensified their anti-government demonstrations in Jakarta in March. Foreign Min. Subandrio increasingly became the target of the demonstrators for his alleged opposition to the anti-PKI drive in 1965 and for his purported pro-Communist sympathies. Massive protest rallies were held in front of Subandrio's offices Mar. 1, 3 and 5. Police on all 3 occasions thwarted attempts by the demonstrators to invade Subandrio's offices. Student rioters Mar. 8 succeeded in storming Subandrio's working quarters. They tossed furniture and files out the window and burned them. Police then fired in the air and dispersed the intruders.

Sukarno Yields Powers to Suharto

The violent anti-government demonstrations led to the first of a series of major shifts in Indonesia's government structure Mar. 12, 1966. Sukarno that day bowed to an army ultimatum and turned over virtually all his government powers to Lt. Gen. Suharto, army commander. Suharto's first act was to ban the PKI.

Foreign Min. Subandrio and 14 other leftwing cabinet members were placed under military detention. Among those detained: 3d Deputy Premier Chaerul Saleh, Information Min. Achmadi, Basic Education Min. Sumardjo, Nationalist Party leader Ali Sastroamidjojo, Electricity & Power Min. Setiadi, Central Bank Min. Yusof Muda Dalam and Minister without Portfolio Surachman, secretary general of the Nationalist Party. Oei Tjat, presidium assistant, was said to have been wounded while resisting detention.

Suharto explained Mar. 18 that the 15 ministers had been placed under protective custody to make certain that they "did not fall victim to unbridled action by certain groups" angered at their alleged involvement in the 1965 abortive coup.

Suharto and Nasution had met with other military leaders earlier in March and lined up support against Sukarno. Acting for Suharto, Brig. Gen. Amir Machmud, Jakarta garrison commander, handed Sukarno Mar. 11 an ultimatum demanding that he dismiss Subandrio and turn over government powers to the army Mar. 12 because the military could not take responsibility for public safety in view of the anti-government riots. The generals were said to have apprised Sukarno of their possession of a document, purportedly signed by Subandrio and Chinese Communist Foreign Min. Chen Yi, that called for the assassination of Nasution and other anti-Communist generals in return for Peking's support for Sukarno's proposed Conference of New Emerging Forces. The military ultimatum was backed by a strong show of force when pro-Suharto troops of the Siliwangi Division moved into Jakarta and took up strategic positions in the city. At a cabinet meeting Mar. 12 Sukarno capitulated to the army ultimatum and signed a document handing over virtually all his government powers to Suharto.

There was only one reported outbreak of fighting during the army takeover. Paratroopers sent to Subandrio's office Mar. 12 to collect his official files exchanged gunfire with intelligence service forces who refused to turn over the material. The intelligence force surrendered after the clash, and the files were confiscated.

The Mar. 12 government change-over was followed Mar. 27 by the formation of a 29-minister cabinet under the influence of the Indonesian armed forces. The new ruling group, replacing a 95-member cabinet, was set up after Sukarno had negotiated since Mar. 16 with Gen. Suharto. Sukarno retained his titles of president, commander-in-chief of the armed forces, great leader of the revolution and premier. Sukarno installed the new ministers and their 30 deputies Mar. 30.

In an address after the swearing-in ceremonies, Sukarno insisted that he had appointed the ministers without outside interference. "I am not a figurehead president," he insisted. Sukarno declared Apr. 7 that he was "still in power" despite moves to reduce his authority. "I am still president and premier and I have not been ousted or toppled," he said.

The new ministerial appointees included a 6-member presidium (inner cabinet), which Sukarno said would "carry out daily affairs at my directive." Gen. Nasution returned to the cabinet as minister and deputy supreme commander of the Crush Malaysia Command. With the exception of Suharto, the 6-man presidium included all the appointees Suharto had announced Mar. 18 after the ouster of Subandrio and the 14 other pro-leftist cabinet ministers. Ex-2d Deputy Premier Johannes Leimena became first deputy premier in charge of the presidium and general affairs; Moslem Scholar Party leader Kiai Haji Idham Chalid became 2d deputy premier in charge of the State Executive Council; ex-Public Affairs Min. Ruslan Abdulgani became 3d deputy premier in charge of political affairs; Hamengku Buwono became 4th deputy premier in charge of economy, finance and development; Suharto became 5th deputy premier in charge of defense and security; ex-Trade Min. Adam Malik (former head of the leftwing Murba party) became 6th deputy premier in charge of foreign affairs and social affairs. (Foreign Min. Malik Mar. 22 had dismissed 2 Subandrio aides—First Deputy Foreign Min. Ganis Harsono and 2d Deputy Foreign Min. [Mrs.] Supeni. Malik announced that Indonesia would pursue an "independent and active" foreign policy, "independent of East and West.")

The anti-government demonstrations had ceased and Jakarta returned to normal following the ouster and seizure of the 15 ministers. Jakarta radio announced Mar. 19 that Suharto had ordered the reopening Mar. 21 of schools and universities that had been closed during the 3 weeks of unrest. Jakarta's civilian airport was reopened to international flights. But the new cabinet and Sukarno's indefinite term as president were assailed Mar. 30 by several thousand university students in a Jakarta demonstration led by the anti-Communist Student Action Front. The students insisted on strict adherence to provisions of the constitution that called for a 5-year limit on the presidency and that provided for a vice president as the president's legal successor.

Congress Reduces Sukarno's Powers

The 520-member Provisional People's Consultative Congress convened in Jakarta June 20, 1966 and voted July 5 to strip Sukarno of his title of "president for life." (The congress had bestowed the title in 1963.) The body also authorized Gen. Suharto to serve as acting president if Sukarno were ill or out of the country.

In a sweeping series of unanimously adopted resolutions, interpreted as reducing Sukarno's status to that of a figure-head, the congress also: (1) authorized Suharto to form a new cabinet by Aug. 17 to replace Sukarno's 90-member cabinet; (2) stipulated that an election be held by July 5, 1968; (3) stripped Sukarno of his power to issue decrees; (4) ordered a review of all decrees issued by Sukarno since July 5, 1959 (when he reinstated the 1945 constitution) and a review of all laws adopted by parliament; (5) ordered the dissolution of all state institutions not enumerated in the constitution; (6) called for legislation on political parties aimed at "simplifying political life."

In other resolutions, designed to shift the course of Indo-nesia's foreign policies, the Congress: (1) recommended to parliament that Indonesia rejoin the UN, the International Monetary Fund and the International Bank for Reconstruction & Development; (2) favored a resolution of Indonesia's dis-pute with Malaysia; (3) declared that Indonesia should follow a "free and independent" course in foreign relations; (4) for-bade the spread of Communist ideology in Indonesia except for the teaching of Marxism and Leninism in university courses on history or political science.

The Congress June 21 had unanimously approved Sukarno's Mar. 12 decree turning over emergency power to Suharto; the decree was to remain effective until general elections took place. In a speech to the congress June 22, Sukarno chal-lenged its authority to elect a president and vice president. The speech was sharply criticized by many Congress delegates June 23 and was attacked by the Intellectuals Action Front in a statement, presented June 24 to Nasution, calling for Sukarno's immediate resignation.

Suharto Heads Cabinet Presidium

The formation of a 27-man cabinet and a 5-man cabinet

presidium headed by Gen. Suharto as chairman was announced by Sukarno July 25, 1966. Suharto said he had accepted the chairmanship of the presidium to implement Sukarno's Mar. 11 decree granting Suharto emergency powers to rule the country.

In forming the new cabinet, Suharto excluded most of Sukarno's close associates. Sukarno kept his additional position of prime minister, and Suharto retained his post as minister of defense and security. The other presidium members were: Foreign Min. Adam Malik (political affairs); Sultan Hamengku Buwono (economic and financial affairs); Kiai Haji Idham Chalid (social affairs); Sanusi Hardjadinata (industrial and development affairs). Suharto, Malik, Buwono and Chalid had been deputy premiers in the previous cabinet. 2 other former deputy premiers (and close associates of Sukarno) — Johannes Leimena and Ruslan Abdulgani — were not taken into the new cabinet.

Coup Leaders Sentenced to Death

3 alleged leaders of the 1965 abortive coup were convicted and sentenced to death at a series of trials held by an Extraordinary Military Tribunal in Jakarta in 1966. Those sentenced were Njono bin Sastroedjo, a leading PKI official, Lt. Col. Untung, a battalion commander in Sukarno's bodyguard, and ex-Air Vice Marshal Omar Dhani.

Njono went on trial Feb. 14 and was convicted and sentenced to death Feb. 21. Njono was reported to have told the court Feb. 14 that the PKI had staged the revolt to keep a group of army generals from seizing power. Njono was quoted as saying: In Aug. 1965 he had attended 3 meetings at which the generals had discussed their plans. The PKI concluded from these meetings that the army's plan called for seizing the government, ousting the cabinet and replacing it with military men. Njono had informed Sukarno of the alleged generals' plot.

Untung went on trial Feb. 23 and was convicted and sentenced to death Mar. 7. In testimony Feb. 25 Untung confessed that he had initiated the coup to thwart a plot by the alleged council of generals to depose Sukarno and take power. Maj. Kusmandi, testifying Feb. 26 for Untung said Sukarno had been given a tape recording of a Sept. 21, 1965 meeting of generals at which the officers had plotted to overthrow Sukarno and to appoint Gen. Nasution, then defense minister, as premier.

Jakarta radio said Feb. 27 that the Sept. 21 meeting, attended by more than 200 officers, had been called only to discuss military training.

Dhani went on trial Dec. 5 and was convicted and sentenced to death Dec. 24. Testimony given at his trial had implicated Sukarno in the attempted Communist coup. Dhani had said that Sukarno had congratulated Brig. Gen. Supardjo, who had engineered the kidnaping and slaying of 6 generals in Jakarta during the uprising. According to other testimony at the trial: Sukarno had agreed to a plan to import 100,000 small weapons from Communist China for Communist-trained guerrillas in Indonesia; Sukarno had agreed to hide Dhani at his Bogor palace one day after the attempted coup, although there was strong evidence that Dhani had been implicated in the uprising; Sukarno had voiced opposition to the appointment of Suharto as temporary army commander and, instead, had appointed a general who later turned out to be pro-Communist.

Sukarno Linked to Coup

The testimony at Omar Dhani's trial intensified public demands that Sukarno give an account of his policies that had led to the attempted Communist coup and of his failure to prevent the uprising when he allegedly knew of the plans. Anti-Sukarno rallies had been staged by students in Jakarta Dec. 20-21, 1966. A resolution submitted Dec. 20 by students and other "action fronts" to the Supreme Court and the attorney general demanded that Sukarno be "dishonorably dismissed" and be put on trial. Foreign Min. Adam Malik expressed hope Dec. 30 that Sukarno would meet "the people's demands" in 1967 for an explanation of his political actions.

Increasing charges that he was connected with the abortive coup prompted Sukarno to issue a statement of denial June 10, 1967. In a message sent to the Provisional People's Consultative Congress, Sukarno said the attempted coup had been "a complete surprise to me." He said his investigations of the episode had "indicated" that it had been the result of the Communist leadership's following "the wrong way" and of the "cunning of 'nekolism [neocolonialism, colonialism and imperialism]' subversion." Referring to the Congressional demand that he give an account of his official actions, Sukarno said he would answer questions posed by the Congressional leadership, although he regarded their request as being "beyond the broad lines of the polity of the state." Sukarno deplored the fact that he was the only one singled out by Congress. He asked why Nasution, who had been coordinating minister for security at the time of the coup attempt, was not "responsible, too." Sukarno complained that it was unfair to hold him alone responsible for Indonesia's economic deterioration.

An article published Jan. 23 by the official Armed Forces Information Center charged that Sukarno has "maintained a direct relationship" with the 1965 Communist plotters. The article said: Sukarno had been informed of the planned Communist uprising a day before it was to have taken place. Sukarno had summoned the military leader of the plot, Brig. Gen. Supardjo, and ordered him not to surrender to the troops that were to suppress the uprising.

The House of Representatives Feb. 9 approved a resolution calling on the Congress to dismiss Sukarno and to try him on charges of complicity in the coup attempt and on charges of corruption. The Congress' standing committee Feb. 17 approved the House resolution and decided to convene Congress Mar. 7 to consider actions against Sukarno.

A decision handed down by the Indonesian Supreme Court Feb. 13 had also recommended that Congress put Sukarno on trial. The tribunal charged that Sukarno had stolen $7 million and had deposited some of the money in banks in Tokyo and Amsterdam. The court claimed that Sukarno had "prior knowledge and understanding" of the Communist coup attempt and that he had given "protection to leaders of the coup against legal action."

Sukarno Relinquishes More Powers

Sukarno surrendered his remaining executive powers to Gen. Suharto Feb. 20, 1967. Sukarno however retained his title as president. The transfer of power was first disclosed Feb. 22 by Information Min. B. M. Diah following a brief cabinet presidium meeting. Diah said the decision to cede full governmental authority to Suharto had been stated in a document signed by Sukarno. In his statement, Sukarno called "on the entire Indonesian people, [and] the leaders . . ., to uphold the revolution" and to back Suharto. Sukarno said he had decided to relinquish his powers "fully realizing that the political conflict that has arisen must quickly be brought to an end for the safety of the Indonesian people and the state."

The transfer of power, Sukarno explained, was in accordance with the July 5, 1966 decision of the Provisional People's Consultative Congress, which had stipulated that "if the president is indisposed," Suharto "holds the post of acting president." Sukarno's statement said, however, that Suharto was required to "report to the president on matters pertaining to the transfer of authority at any time."

In a speech to parliament Mar. 4 Suharto said that Sukarno had initiated the move to give up his executive powers with the full approval of the armed forces commanders.

Sukarno's decision to relinquish power was reported Feb. 25 to have precipitated clashes between pro- and anti-Sukarno factions. 6 persons were reported killed and 13 injured when a Moslem anti-Sukarno mob, armed with swords and knives, attacked a police post at Pemalang, Central Java; police fired at the Moslems. Pro-Sukarno youths, clad in black uniforms and red berets, wrecked the printing plant of the anti-Sukarno newspaper *Merdeka (Freedom)* in Surabaya, East Java; according to the army newspaper *Berit Yudha*, they also attacked a high school and beat students. In Jogjakarta, Java, pro-Sukarno youths attacked the regional Legislative Assembly as it debated a resolution for Sukarno's ouster; policemen quelled the disturbance.

Sukarno Loses All Powers; Suharto Acting President

The 653-member Provisional People's Consultative Congress convened in special session Mar. 7, 1967 and unanimously approved a resolution Mar. 12 stripping Sukarno of all executive and ceremonial powers and temporarily barring him from participating in political activities. The resolution appointed Gen. Suharto acting president pending presidential elections in 1968.

Sukarno was permitted to retain his title of president, but a 2d resolution deprived him of the right to call himself "Great Leader of the Revolution."

The resolution approved by the Congress: "revokes the mandate of the Congress to Pres. Sukarno and all governmental powers accorded him by the Constitution of 1945"; "forbids Pres. Sukarno to carry out any political activities until the time of the general elections," scheduled for 1968; appointed Suharto acting president until after Congressional elections but held Suharto to be "subordinate and accountable" to Congress; empowered Suharto to appoint a commission to consider trying Sukarno on charges of being involved in the 1965 coup attempt and of diverting public funds; established a committee to review Sukarno's 1959 Political Manifesto, on which he had based his principle of guided democracy.

Suharto had warned the Congress at its opening session Mar. 7 not to take drastic action against Sukarno lest it cause "physical conflict in the country" and split the armed forces. Suharto also defended Sukarno's actions during the attempted 1965 coup. Suharto said Sukarno was aware of threatening violence then, "but he did not know positively of the impending coup." Sukarno had not acted against the Communists after the attempted coup nor in defense of them "but for safeguarding his own political concepts," Suharto said. Suharto said Mar. 13 that because of Sukarno's failing health he would, "for the time being," "be treated as president but without any power and authority whatsoever."

The Indonesian cabinet May 10 stripped Sukarno of his title of chief of state and barred him from using his former titles of president, supreme commander of the armed forces and mandatory of the People's Consultative Congress. The cabinet also ordered Sukarno to leave the Presidential Palace in Jakarta, which he had occupied since 1945.

Supardjo Captured and Sentenced to Death

Ex-Brig. Gen. Supardjo, sought since the 1965 abortive coup, was arrested Jan. 12, 1967 near the Halim air base outside Jakarta. Military officers were said to have confessed that they had concealed Supardjo after he had produced orders from Sukarno requesting that he be protected. Also seized with Supardjo was Anwar Sanusi, identified as a PKI leader.

Supardjo went on trial before a military tribunal in Jakarta Feb. 23. He was convicted and sentenced to death Mar. 13 on charges of having led troops against the government in the coup attempt. Supardjo testified during the trial that the attempted coup was not a Communist plot aimed at overthrowing the government. Supardjo said he and other officers belonging to the Sept. 30th Movement had actually sought to prevent a coup planned by the rightwing "council of generals." Supardjo denied that he was one of the principal planners of the movement. He said that advice he had given the dissident army officers had been ignored.

(Another close aide of Sukarno's, ex-3d Deputy Premier Chaerul Saleh, 50, had died in prison in Jakarta Feb. 8. Saleh had been seized in Mar. 1966. He had been awaiting trial on charges of corruption and of involvement in the planned uprising.)